The Incredible Indoor Games Book

160 Group Projects, Games, and Activities

Bob Gregson

Fearon Teacher Aids
Carthage, Illinois

To my parents, Bob and Alda, who showed me the importance of play — and my friend, Bernie DeKoven, who helped me to appreciate it and whose efforts made this book possible.

Acknowledgments

The Incredible Indoor Games Book owes its existence to many playful people. Thanks to:

Donald Clark for the original format;

Bernie DeKoven for his games — Kung Thumb, Living Clay, World Champion Paper-Stacking Contest, Multiple Hopscotch, Box Links, Stacking the Deck, Nice Big Dice, Group Loop — and many more ideas and play days;

Tom Zink for our many collaborations which resulted from our Mistake Practices, plus many game ideas, especially Human Mixmaster and Zink Vortex;

Sandy Cohen for her games — Lean and Leave, Real-Life Drama, and Ripples (invented with *Debbie Addis*);

Dic Wheeler for Reincarnator;

Gary Andreadis and the *Music Seminar* for Jam Session and Creating Silence;

Bill Derry and *Marione Cobb* for finding a few more games;

the *Oddfellows Players* for their continued support;

the *New Haven Teacher's Center* for being a unique and special resource;

the *Boston Children's Museum Resource Center*;

Chris, Mark, and Judy — my brothers and sister — for playing along with me; and

Buff Bradley for introducing me to a new playground.

Editorial director: Roberta Suid
Editor: Buff Bradley
Production manager: Suzanne Olver
Text and cover designer: Susan True
Illustrator: Bob Gregson
Manufacturing manager: Susan Fox

Library of Congress Catalog Card Number: 82-81983
ISBN-0-8224-0765-5
Printed in the United States of America.

CONTENTS

INTRODUCTION

Indoor play can be varied, surprising, active, engaging, stimulating, creative, and plenty of fun. These 160 projects, games, and activities are all designed for indoor group play. Some are variations of traditional games; some are brand new; all are simple enough to learn quickly and yet substantial enough to invite repeated playings and any number of revisions and variations. Most are appropriate for use with kids from age six to sixteen, with slight adjustments for the skill levels of players.

Each of the games and activities falls into one of three categories — Spur of the Moment, A Little Preparation, and Plan Ahead — according to the preparation necessary.

SPUR OF THE MOMENT

Spur of the Moment games and activities are ones you'll be able to insert into a schedule at the last minute — when a surprise storm makes outdoor play impossible or tension and energy levels strongly suggest an *ad hoc* diversion. None of them uses any materials; most take ten to twenty minutes to play; a few require some room rearrangement.

A LITTLE PREPARATION

A little preparation is all it will take to prepare for these games and activities. They use materials readily available in schools, homes, and offices — paper, pencils, felt-tipped markers, and string. Again, most do not take up too much time — twenty to thirty minutes at most — and can be done without rearranging a classroom or an activities room.

PLAN AHEAD

Cardboard boxes, rolls of foil, long bolts of fabric, and video equipment are some of the materials you'll need for games and activities in the Plan Ahead section. These materials must be gathered beforehand, so you will have to do some planning as well as a little scrounging. (After a Plan Ahead activity has been done once, however, materials can stay near at hand and be used again at a moment's notice.) In most cases, the materials will define activities as players investigate possible uses and effect transformations. Most of the Plan Ahead games and activities are more complicated than those in the other two parts of the book and require more play time — usually thirty to sixty minutes.

THE VALUE OF PLAY

Although the spirit of play is impossible to define, the value of play is clear. The opportunities for play in this book serve a number of important purposes beyond just plain fun.

Problem Solving

Each activity has a structure and an objective which exercise problem-solving skills. Players analyze the problem an activity presents and explore various solutions. In exploring ways to build an arch with boxes, stack folded sheets of paper into towers, or discover the identity of a secret leader, players learn to adapt, modify, and sharpen ideas.

Imagination and Spontaneity

We all see and interpret the world in our own unique ways. Children develop their own visions as they act out fantasies, invent sounds and movements, and create worlds of color and shape. Activities provide opportunities to respond creatively and spontaneously to structured situations, and to explore the uniqueness of their imaginations.

Cooperation, Socialization, and Collaboration

To make a game work, players must work together. A game such as Group Juggle works best when everyone concentrates on keeping his or her part of the activity moving. Problem-solving activities require the participation and ideas of all members. When a group plays problem-solving games successfully, it creates an atmosphere of trust in which the contribution of each player is sought and valued.

MAKING FUN

"No, that's boring!" To find the fun in all the games and activities in this book, you may have to make adjustments to fit the abilities, interests, and needs of your group. When contemplating changes, consider the following elements.

Players

The number of players can affect an activity tremendously. A tag game with five people is quite different from a tag game with fifty-five people. If a game with a large group gets too chaotic, divide into smaller groups or several teams. If certain games become too dull, heighten the challenge by selecting more than one person to be It.

Room

The limitations of a room (size, furniture, the group next door, and so forth) can be frustrating and may require that certain rules be altered. If noise is a problem, pick a game in which being quiet is the challenge or add a "no talking" rule to a game that doesn't necessarily require silence. If the room is crowded with desks and chairs, try to incorporate them as boundaries, obstacles, or building blocks. The visual qualities (color, shape, lighting, and so forth) set a psychological tone which affects the mood and spirit of players. Propose an activity to pep up a dull room — decorating walls and ceilings with banners, flags, murals, or posters.

Time

Add time limitations to create additional challenge and excitement as players strive to find a solution and beat the clock. Relax time limitations if they create frustration and turn what could be an exciting game into an impossible obstacle course.

Materials

Changing the materials can transform a game or activity completely. Playing baseball with an eight-foot carpet tube and a balloon creates a whole new game. Building towers with paper instead of wooden blocks becomes an engineering problem of an entirely different order. Don't be afraid to substitute materials for any of the activities. Invite suggestions about what substitutions would be fun and challenging.

Rules

Rules are the central structure of every game. They create the problems players seek to solve. If one rule is changed it will effect every other rule, and eventually redefine the game. For example, a "no hands" rule for playing tag means a new method of tagging must be devised — possibly with noses, feet, or elbows. In this case, further rules are necessary so that players don't kick each other and noses don't get broken.

In order to play, everyone must agree on the rules and any changes must be ratified by the entire group. If everyone agrees to bend one rule — to peek for five seconds, to take another turn, or to skip a turn — to make the game more enjoyable, then by all means do it. If bending a rule bothers you, try borrowing a rule (everyone is safe in the free zone, you can't be tagged while hugging someone, you have three seconds to answer, and so on), thus creating a hybrid of games. Remember, rules are for the convenience of those playing. Rules that work at one time may be inhibiting at another. If changing a rule or two isn't enough to pep up the activity, change the game by adopting an entirely new set of rules.

Scoring

Most of the games and activities in *The Incredible Indoor Games Book* don't involve keeping score. Keeping score in games can have a negative as well as a positive effect. There are times, however, when interest begins to wane. To increase the challenge and perk up the interest, play for a score. When scoring is used to encourage each player to play better rather than to prove that one player is better than another, then it is serving its purpose. When keeping score becomes more important than playing the game, scorekeeping should be abandoned and the game reformulated into a cooperative rather than a competitive event.

It is amazing how differently games are played when the reasons for scoring change. Traditionally, points are awarded for "fastest" and "most." But points can also be given for innovation, imagination, endurance, style, and agility. Brainstorm to come up with novel scoring systems. For some games, you may simply invert the traditional system. For example, winners of a relay race are those that finish last, not first — but everybody has to keep moving. This reversal gives the race a new feel and creates a brand new challenge. For some games you may try awarding points for cooperation. Teams that involve all members get extra points; teams on which one or two members take charge and leave others out lose points. In activities such as paper airplane contests, you can give points not only to the best fliers and the most innovative designs, but also to the strangest plane or even the funniest one. Always be on the lookout for ways to use scoring that encourage players rather than discourage them.

PART ONE
Spur of the Moment

At the last minute you find that the plans you made won't work. Now's the time for one of the following spur-of-the-moment games and activities. The fun can start almost instantly because the games need very few materials and call for few or no special room arrangements. Some space may be needed for players to stand in a circle or to sit on the floor. Most of these activities are short—many less than ten minutes — and can be fun without any planning.

Theater Games

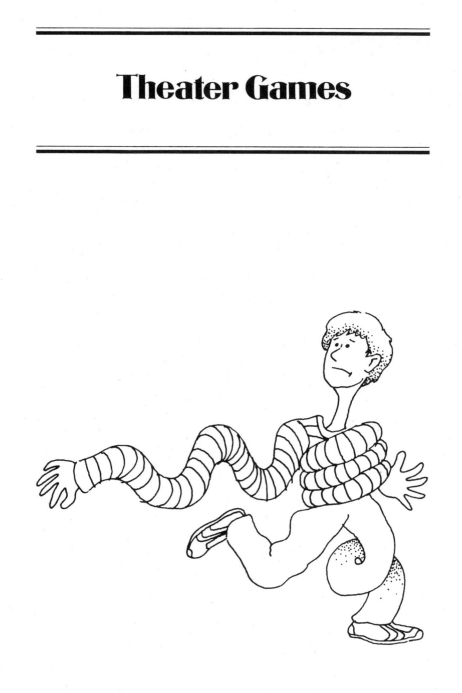

PROUDLY PRESENTING

What could be more perfect than having
someone tell everyone how wonderful you are?
Why just dream about it?

MATERIALS

None

ROOM ARRANGEMENT

Open space

TIME

15 minutes

DIRECTIONS

   1. Players find partners. Preferably, people who don't know each other
very well should pair up.

   2. Partners have five minutes to tell things that they would like the other
to know about their lives — hobbies; accomplishments; favorite foods,
places, and things; plans for the future; and so forth.

   3. Players sit in a circle, but partners do not sit next to each other. In turn,
players stand and introduce their partners. For example, "I am very happy
to say that we have an expert guitar player with us today. He likes to fish,
swim, and eat chocolate-chip ice cream sundaes. May I present to you
Dennis Myers!" The person introduced stands up and bows as the group
applauds and cheers.

LET'S FACE IT

People need little or no excuse to indulge in making faces. Here's a way to make a funny face game.

MATERIALS
None

ROOM ARRANGEMENT
Open space

TIME
20 minutes

DIRECTIONS

1. Push all furniture aside. Have everyone sit in a circle on the floor. The object of the game is to make the funniest face possible.

2. A short demonstration of everyone's funny face will set the tone for the game. Have players inflate cheeks, wrinkle noses, furrow eyebrows, show teeth, and so forth.

3. This game works well as a fantasy. Tell players that a magic spell has been cast over the group, changing everyone's face. To save everyone from the spell, a funny face must pass around the entire group, person to person, until it gets back to the first person again. Then, magically, the spell will vanish!

4. After everyone has practiced making faces, the leader begins slowly changing his or her face into a funny expression, then turns slowly to a neighbor who must mirror the face.

5. The second person, after mirroring the leader's expression, changes the face as he or she turns to the third person. The third person mirrors the face, changes it, and passes it on around the entire circle.

6. The last person passes a funny face to the leader, who mirrors it and slowly changes his or her face back to normal, thus breaking the spell and saving the group.

OUT-OF-SIGHT SHAPES

What would happen if, without warning, you pulled a five-foot banana from your pocket and began to peel it? Well, you can — anytime — with invisible shapes. In this game the players' imaginations become the props.

MATERIALS

None

ROOM ARRANGEMENT

Open space

TIME

15 minutes

DIRECTIONS

1. Clear an area of the room. Have everyone stand in a circle.
2. This game is a pantomime in which an invisible piece of space can be squeezed, squashed, twisted, or rolled into any imaginable object. To begin, quietly pull a chunk of invisible space out of your pocket or from behind your back. Continue to expand it into a large pretend object, such as a fishing pole or an oversized baseball bat. Transform your invisible object into another form, and then pass it along to the next person.
3. Each player should take about thirty seconds to transform the shape from a ball to a balloon to a hat — anything! After finishing, each player passes the shape along to the next player.
4. When the invisible shape gets back to you, treat it carefully in order to maintain its mysteriousness. Gently squeeze it back into a small ball and put it away so that it can be used again at some other time.

LEAN AND LEAVE

This playful mime technique teaches players an invaluable lesson in self-reliance — their own support system!

MATERIALS

None

ROOM ARRANGEMENT

Open space

TIME

10 minutes

DIRECTIONS

   1. Players choose partners. The object of the game is for players to look as if they're leaning, but actually to be able to stand without support.
   2. One partner leans on the shoulder of the other. The leaning player then shifts weight slightly so that he or she is actually standing alone.
   3. When leaning players can lean unsupported, they say "OK" to their partners, who move away, leaving them looking as if they were leaning on thin air.
   4. After both partners have leaned alone, divide players into groups of three with two players leaning on a middle player. When the middle player moves, the two others will look as if they were chatting away and didn't notice the support was missing.

INVISIBLE TUG-OF-WAR

Some tug-of-war games depend on pure muscle. In this version players must use their imagination muscles.

MATERIALS

None

ROOM ARRANGEMENT

Open space

TIME

10 minutes

DIRECTIONS

1. Two players are chosen to stand in front of the group and pretend they are tugging a rope back and forth — just like the original version.

2. As the two tuggers pantomime pulling the rope, one will begin to lose. When a player looks as if he or she is losing, one person from the group hops up to help out.

3. One by one, players from the group continue to add themselves to the losing team until eventually both teams are filled.

4. It may not seem possible, but as in all tug-of-war games, the stronger team will win.

WALK MY WALK

Close observation will reveal that no two people walk in the same manner. This game investigates all walks of life.

MATERIALS

None

ROOM ARRANGEMENT

Open space

TIME

15 minutes

DIRECTIONS

1. Have players stand in a circle with plenty of space in the middle. Discuss the many ways people walk. For example, a spy might creep along on tiptoes while a fashion model walks with a studied, erect posture.

2. Players select a role with a specific kind of walk. Some ideas are:

- tightrope walker
- astronaut on the moon
- window washer on a ledge
- infant learning to walk
- old person
- body builder
- marching soldier
- circus clown
- explorer at the North Pole

3. Each player walks across the circle several times as the group tries to guess his or her identity. When someone guesses correctly, the entire group imitates the walk, then forms into a circle again to watch another walk.

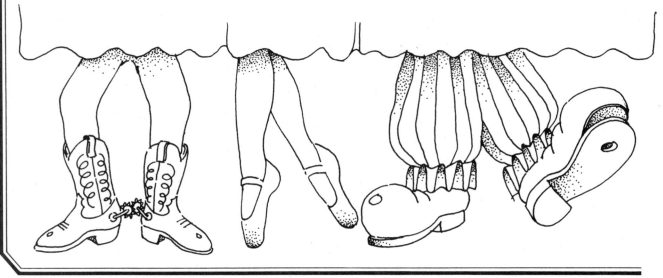

ANIMAL, BIRD, OR FISH

Players will be flying high, sailing along, and climbing the walls with this pantomime game.

MATERIALS

None

ROOM ARRANGEMENT

Open space

TIME

15 minutes

DIRECTIONS

1. Divide players into two teams. Teams position themselves in corners of the room opposite each other. A leader is chosen to stand in the center — equal distance from each team.

2. Each team sends one player to the leader in the middle who whispers to each the name of an animal, bird, or fish. If the leader says *monkey,* for example, each player runs back to his or her team, to act out a monkey in pantomime.

3. When a team member guesses *monkey* the pantomiming player runs back and touches the leader, saying "Monkey!" The first player back to the leader is the winner.

PASSING THE BUCK

Players won't have to buck this system — they just pass it along.

MATERIALS

A glove, a beanbag, a small rubber ball, or any other tossable object

ROOM ARRANGEMENT

Open space

TIME

15 minutes

DIRECTIONS

1. Have everyone stand in a circle. The "buck" is any small object that can be tossed easily from player to player — a glove, a beanbag, or a rubber ball.

2. Toss the buck to a player in the circle. The person catching the buck must begin to tell a story — something made up on the spot.

3. The player holding the buck tosses it to another player who must catch it and continue the story. The story can take any form just as long as there is an attempt to connect it to the last player's contribution.

4. Players must not break the flow of the story no matter how fast the buck is passed. Those who have the buck must speak — if only a few words — and then they can toss it to another.

Once upon a time....

CLOSE CALLS

This game is based on the old familiar game of Telephone, but you won't find these variations in any phone book.

MATERIALS

None

ROOM ARRANGEMENT

Open space

TIME

15 minutes

DIRECTIONS

1. In the oldest form of the game Telephone, players sit in a straight line while the person at one end whispers a brief message to the next person.

2. The second player whispers the message to the third person who, in turn, whispers it to the fourth person.

3. The story makes its way down the line to the end. The final person repeats the message aloud. It will likely bear little resemblance to the original. You can count on at least one person to distort it dramatically.

VARIATIONS

- Gather everyone in a circle. Instead of passing a single message around in one direction, try passing two messages in opposite directions.
- Have many people pass messages at the same time. Have players sit in a circle and count off alternately — "one" and "two." To begin, each "one" whispers a message to the "two" on the right. Next, the "twos" pass the messages along so many messages are being passed at once. The messages go around the entire circle until they return to the originators. Players tell their messages in both the original and altered versions.

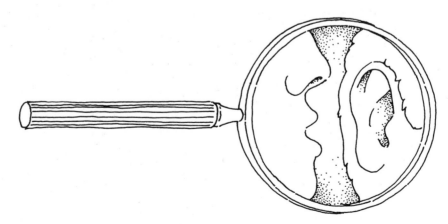

REAL-LIFE DRAMA

"Real life is the stuff of drama." Or is it "Drama is the stuff of real life"? In this game dramatic real-life experiences become dramatic dramas.

MATERIALS

None

ROOM ARRANGEMENT

Open space

TIME

45 minutes

DIRECTIONS

1. Players sit in a circle on the floor and tell the most interesting, dramatic thing that has happened to them — getting lost, playing in an exciting ball game, rescuing an ailing bird, being in an accident, riding in a parade — something that was exciting, scary, or unusual. Set a one-minute time limit on each player's story.

2. After everyone has told a story, divide the groups into smaller groups of five or six. Each group selects several elements from each person's story that can be combined into a short skit. Encourage imaginative combinations, such as picking up a baby bird while crossing the goal line for the winning touchdown.

3. Each group takes a turn to perform its skit for everyone.

NOW THE NEWS

After you've played Telephone, you know how stories change dramatically as they are passed from person to person. In this game players pretend they are on-the-spot reporters adding to a news story as it unfolds without any planning.

MATERIALS

None

ROOM ARRANGEMENT

Chairs in a circle

TIME

15 minutes

DIRECTIONS

1. Get everyone seated in a comfortable position in a circle. The object of this game is for each player to add three words to a single story as it is passed around the group. The three words should help describe an incredible news story. The more absurd the funnier.

2. Begin the story slowly. For example, the first player might say "Late last night . . ."; the second player might add ". . . a green monster . . ."; while the next player adds ". . . ate New York." If someone gets stuck and can't think of something, come back later. It is important to keep the game moving along from player to player.

VARIATION

Select a simple object such as a paper bag, a key, a piece of string — anything that can be passed around. As it is being passed around the group, have each player add three words to its life story. Allow each person's imagination to unravel as the object's family, friends, and travels are discussed.

OUTRIGHT LIE

This game should turn up the most inventive and believable storyteller in the group. Everyone will get a chance to tell the most far-out stories in as truthful a manner as possible.

MATERIALS

A key, a ring, a pencil, scissors, or any other small object

ROOM ARRANGEMENT

As is

TIME

25 minutes

DIRECTIONS

1. Select a small object such as a key, a ring, a pencil, or scissors. Players should be seated in their usual places and pass the object from person to person.

2. As the object is passed around the room, each player must come up with an incredible story or fantasy to tell to the rest of the group. For example, if a key is selected, the stories might sound like this: "This key unlocks a treasure worth more than Fort Knox, a treasure located 14 miles below the surface of the Atlantic Ocean." Or: "This key saved the life of a man when it stopped a bullet while he was fighting in a war."

3. After everyone has finished, ask the group members which lie they enjoyed the most. The person with the most entertaining lie may have the dubious honor of being the least-trusted person in the group.

FACT OR FICTION

In this game, style is just as important as content. Players tell plausible fictions or outrageous facts and guess which is which.

MATERIALS
None

ROOM ARRANGEMENT
Open space

TIME
20 minutes

DIRECTIONS

1. Have everyone sit in a circle. The object of the game is to try to tell a true story that sounds like a lie or a lie that sounds like a true story.

2. Players take turns relating true or imaginary information about themselves or their families. The leader should set the tone by giving an example: "I have a pet swan that always makes my mother sneeze because she's allergic to its feathers."

3. After each turn the group must judge — fact or fiction. If a person is lying and the group thinks it's the truth, or if the person is telling the truth and the group thinks it's a lie, the person wins. However, if the person is telling the truth or a lie and the group guesses it correctly, the group wins. Remember truth is often stranger than fiction, so lying isn't always necessary.

VARIATION

Do the same project in writing and exchange papers.

TRANSFORMATIONS

With this game, the leader can instantly change a group of players into a jumbo jet!

MATERIALS

None

ROOM ARRANGEMENT

Open space

TIME

15 minutes

DIRECTIONS

1. Divide the group into two teams. The object of the game is for players to form as quickly as possible into human representations of whatever you describe.

2. Call out the name of an object. Team members then must arrange themselves into that shape. For example, if you say *helicopter,* players must decide how they will link together into propellers, cockpit, and landing gear. Other ideas for transformations are suspension bridge, ship, cathedral, capitol dome, tree, waterfall, truck, bus, and skyscraper.

LIVING CLAY

Over the years, artists have used some pretty unusual stuff to make works of art. Here's an art project in which the players become the medium.

MATERIALS

None

ROOM ARRANGEMENT

Open space

TIME

15 minutes

DIRECTIONS

 1. Each person selects a partner. One person becomes a blob of clay, and the other becomes the sculptor.
 2. The sculptor molds and forms the human clay into any shape possible without hurting the clay. Arms can be turned, legs can be bent, heads can be tipped, and faces can be pushed into strange expressions. The clay may resist any unreasonable positions.
 3. When the sculptor is finished, the creation may be put on exhibit. After the exhibit, sculptor and sculpture should switch places.

VARIATION

Divide the entire group into smaller groups of five or six. One person in each group is selected as the sculptor and the others become the clay. The sculptor uses all the others, intertwining limbs and bodies, to form a single sculpture. For a finale, make the world's largest living sculpture using the entire group as clay.

HUMAN MACHINE COMPANY

Machines are useless unless each part is functioning properly. In this activity, groups of players become machines, each player taking the role of one machine part.

MATERIALS
None

ROOM ARRANGEMENT
Open space

TIME
15 minutes

DIRECTIONS

1. Have players form into groups of eight or ten. Each group agrees on a single machine to portray, such as a washing machine, blender, helicopter, lawn mower — anything with moving parts. The object of the activity is to give an impression of a machine and how all the parts work together.

2. One by one, each player pretends to be a machine part and joins the machine. For example, if everyone decides to make a car, then one chugs and shakes to become the engine, another bends over to become the trunk, another stretches arms to become a windshield, and yet another moves arms as windshield wipers.

3. After the machine has been completed, see how well the parts work together. Have each part add a sound; see what different sounds there are when the machine is running at top speed and then at a very slow speed.

4. After each group creates an impression of a specific machine, have the groups reassemble into a totally nonfunctional invention.

TALK SHOW

Did you ever dream you were a very famous person from television or the movies? This game lets people forget about their own personalities and become the famous people they dream about.

MATERIALS

None

ROOM ARRANGEMENT

As is

TIME

15 to 25 minutes

DIRECTIONS

1. Two players leave the room in order to choose two famous characters to portray. Characters can be from real life or fiction, alive or dead, and should be familiar to all or most of the group members. It is usually helpful if the two have some common interest such as music, sports, or politics so that they can carry on a conversation.

2. The two players rejoin the group and begin to have a conversation such as two famous people meeting on a television talk show would have. Warn players not to give each other away with names.

3. The other players try to guess who the two are. Group members who want to guess the two characters' identities do not call out their names, but ask a question directly related to their identity. For example, if one of the famous people is George Washington the question might be "Do you get splinters from your wooden teeth?" If the guess is wrong and the player is not George Washington, he or she might answer "I don't have to use them since my teeth are all real."

4. Players continue to ask questions until many people seem to know the identities of the characters. The leader asks the members of the group who the characters are — and why. Most times the group is in agreement, but at other times each character could be one of several people. The game ends when the group asks the characters to reveal their identities.

LIP SYNC

Have you ever been to a movie that was made in a different language and the English words were dubbed in? If you have, you know that the mouth movements don't always match the words. In this game, the actors pantomime, the dubbers supply the dialogue, and lots of surprises occur.

MATERIALS

None

ROOM ARRANGEMENT

Open space

TIME

30 minutes

DIRECTIONS

1. Four people play at a time. Two are actors and two are dubbers. The rest of the group is the audience.

2. The two actors decide on a real-life drama that includes two characters and a situation. For example:

- Two people on vacation when their car runs out of gas.
- A person smoking a cigarette in a no-smoking zone and a nonsmoker.
- A person in a restaurant who keeps changing the order and an impatient waiter or waitress.
- A door-to-door sales representative trying to sell someone a kangaroo.

The actors and the dubbers work out a very rough plot outline without actually deciding on the dialogue.

3. The actors play out the performance in pantomime. Offstage, the dubbers fill in the words. As the performance progresses, the actors and dubbers eventually affect each other and spontaneous things begin to happen.

4. Switch actors and dubbers frequently. Everyone likes to be onstage so try to give everyone a chance to be an actor or dubber at least once.

IN THE MANNER OF THE ADVERB

Here's a pantomime guessing game that will have everyone hamming it up. Some players do pantomime interpretations of adverbs while others try to guess the words.

MATERIALS

None

ROOM ARRANGEMENT

As is

TIME

20 to 30 minutes

DIRECTIONS

1. One person selected as It leaves the room.
2. The players remaining in the room select an adverb such as *merrily, nervously, warmly,* and so on. The adverb should not be too obvious or too obscure, but difficult enough to cause some thinking.
3. After a word has been agreed upon, the person waiting outside the room can come back and try to guess the word by asking members of the group to perform an action to demonstrate the adverb. For example, he or she might say "Shake hands in the manner of the adverb" or "Walk in the manner of the adverb" or "Look at me in the manner of the adverb."
4. The person who is It keeps on asking for demonstrations until he or she guesses the word. If it becomes too difficult to guess the word and all possibilities have been exhausted, you or the players can give clues to keep the game moving along.

TYPEWRITER

This is truly a manual typewriter with each player in a key role.

MATERIALS

None

ROOM ARRANGEMENT

Open space

TIME

15 minutes

DIRECTIONS

1. Gather everyone in a circle. Each player represents a letter in the alphabet, A through Z. If there are more players than there are letters, one can become a number, another a period, and another an eraser for correcting mistakes.

2. Find or create a sentence that uses all the letters in the alphabet. For example, The quick brown fox jumps over the lazy dog. In the case of extra people it can be 2 dogs.

3. Finally, create a typewriter rhythm for everyone to follow. Everyone claps hands, stamps a foot once, and punches the key by raising a hand in the air. Clap-stamp-punch, clap-stamp-punch — alternating right and left hands and feet.

4. Write the sentence on the chalkboard for everyone to see during the game. The object is to type out the entire sentence using the proper keys without missing a beat. When the typewriter rhythm begins and everyone punches the air, the person with the first letter calls out "T!" When everyone punches the air again, the person with the next letter calls out "H!" On the next punch, the player calls out "E!" When a space between words is reached, everyone calls out together "Space!" If a mistake is made, just keep going, unless there is a person who is the eraser to call out "Correction!"

WORLD PREMIERE

Theater helps utilize our learned responses and makes them visible to us. Many of us are actors from the moment we get up in the morning until we go to sleep at night. This activity uses our unconscious acting abilities in unusual improvised skits.

MATERIALS
Objects found in the room

ROOM ARRANGEMENT
Open space

TIME
30 to 40 minutes

DIRECTIONS
1. Divide players into groups of five.

2. Discuss with everyone the situations to be used as the basis for each group's skit. Suggest something whimsical. For example:

- Cavepeople fixing dinner
- Astronauts on an expedition to Mars encountering Martians
- A world where everything happens backward
- Three fish, a frog, and a turtle living in a polluted river
- An updated fairy tale such as "Goldilocks and the Three Bears" or "The Tortoise and the Hare"

3. After each group has a rough outline, have them find objects in the room as props. The objects can be used as themselves or as substitutes for something else. For example, a broom can be used to sweep or it can become the oar of a boat or the barrel of a gun.

4. As players organize their productions, rearrange furniture into an impromptu stage.

5. When everyone is ready, add a playful air of exaggerated seriousness as you announce the skits. Allow five to ten minutes for each improvised world premiere. As an added touch, have each group take a bow as the rest cheer them on.

Sound and Movement Games

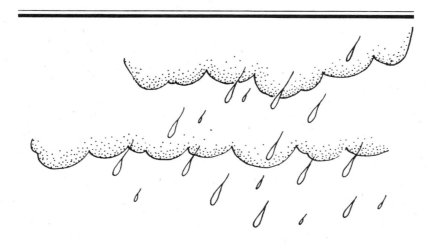

RAIN GAME

In the Rain Game, players create the sound of a rainstorm in the dry and cozy comfort of the indoors.

MATERIALS

None

ROOM ARRANGEMENT

Open space

TIME

10 minutes

DIRECTIONS

1. Everyone stands in a circle. The leader starts by rubbing his or her hands together. The person to the right of the leader joins in, then the next person to the right, then the next, until everyone is doing it. The sound this rubbing makes is much like a soft spray of rain.

2. When all are rubbing their hands, the leader starts a new sound — finger snapping. The rain is gaining in intensity. Each player must continue to rub hands until it is his or her turn to snap fingers.

3. After finger snapping has gone all the way around, the leader begins the next sound — hands slapping thighs.

4. Finally the crescendo of the rainstorm — hands slapping thighs plus foot stomping.

5. To end the rainstorm, completely reverse the activities. The last sound to be passed is the silence as each person, one by one stops rubbing hands.

DUM DUM DA DA

This is a sound and movement game that can be added to continually by those playing it. The instructions may appear complicated, but don't get scared — it's a simple rhythm game.

MATERIALS

None

ROOM ARRANGEMENT

Open space

TIME

15 minutes

DIRECTIONS

1. Have everyone sit on the floor in a circle with their legs crossed, knee touching the knee of the next person. "Dum dum da da" is sung in place of the lyrics for the melody of "Old Man River." Repeat "dum dum da da" eight times with everyone in the group singing along.

2. After you've practiced the song with the group, you're ready to add some movements. On "dum dum," have players slap their own knees twice. On "da da," each player slaps the knee of the person on the right. On the next "dum dum," players slap their own knees twice again, and finally on "da da," each slaps the knee of the person on the left.

3. After everyone has mastered these movements, other movements can be added. Again on "dum dum," players slap their knees twice the regular

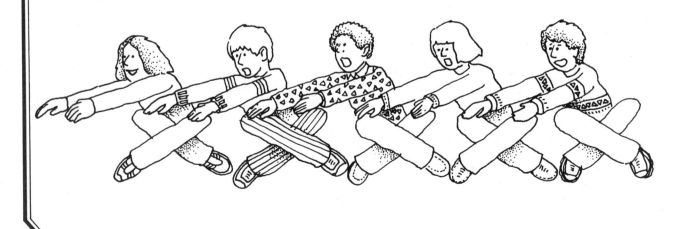

way. On "da da," players cross right arm over left and slap the right knee with the left hand and slap the left knee with the right hand. Then on "dum dum" again, players slap their knees the regular way. Finally on "da da," players cross left arm over right and slap opposite knees.

4. Next, try inventing some of your own movements. Some suggestions:

  • On "dum dum," clap hands twice; on "da da," one player reverses palms and claps the hands of the players on either side.
  or
  • On "dum dum," stomp feet twice on the floor; on "da da," kick legs straight in toward the center of the circle.

5. Dum Dum Da Da can be done standing in a circle. On "dum dum," players turn right and kick twice with their left leg. On "da da," players turn left and kick twice with their right leg. Add arm movements, head movements, and whole body movements.

6. The game continues until players feel they have explored as many movement possibilities as they possibly can.

VARIATION

For smaller children, keep the movements simple and use a melody from a song they know well, such as "Twinkle, Twinkle, Little Star."

RIPPLES

This follow-the-leader-type game is as beautiful to watch as it is to do. It resembles those elaborate movie musicals with lots of dancers creating ever-changing geometric patterns.

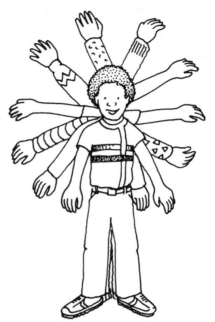

MATERIALS

None

ROOM ARRANGEMENT

Open space

TIME

10 minutes

DIRECTIONS

1. Gather the group into a single line behind the person chosen to be the leader. The object of the game is to follow the movements of the person directly in front of you, rather than following the leader directly.

2. The leader begins a motion that is passed down the line. If the leader raises his or her arm, the second person follows the leader, the third person follows the second, the fourth person follows the third, and so on. The leader does not walk around the room but rather moves arms and legs, bends, leans, and so on, in place.

3. After players have done this a few times, divide the group into two lines with the two leaders facing each other. In this version the second leader mirrors the movements of the first leader. You tell leaders when to switch roles.

4. For the spectacular finale, divide the class into four groups with four leaders facing each other in a big X pattern. Two leaders initiate moves while the other two leaders follow. This version can be used with music to create spectacular dance performances.

JOHNNY WENT TO SLEEP

This is a sound and movement game that, like an old-fashioned slapstick comedy, builds and builds until it is truly a ridiculous sight.

MATERIALS

None

ROOM ARRANGEMENT

Open space

TIME

10 minutes

DIRECTIONS

1. Everyone stands in a circle. The first player begins by saying "Johnny went to sleep." The rest of the group answers "How did Johnny go to sleep?" The leader then says "Johnny went to sleep like this, like this," repeating a small gesture such as nodding the head or twisting the wrist. The rest of the group mimics the gesture and answers "Like this, like this."

2. The entire group continues to repeat the gesture as the next player in line says "Johnny went to sleep," and the others respond as before. The second player adds another gesture to the first, so that now there are two movements to keep going.

3. The game continues around the circle, each player adding a gesture.

4. By the end of the game, the entire group should be a foot-wiggling, eye-blinking, head-shaking, nose-twitching mess. Try to add as many gestures as possible before the game totally falls apart. Since it is difficult to do more than ten gestures at once, you may not get to everyone in the group, but the challenge is to see how far you do get. Start off slowly with small things, such as toes and fingers, and work up to the bigger things, such as arms and legs. But whatever happens, don't get too shook up!

THUMPER

Thumper is a traditional children's game and you've probably played it at some time in your life. Since it's a game that involves memory, groups of eight or ten players work best.

MATERIALS

None

ROOM ARRANGEMENT

Open space

TIME

15 minutes

DIRECTIONS

1. Have the players form groups of eight to ten. Have each group sit on the floor in a circle.

2. Each person must invent a sound and a movement — shaking the head while whistling, winking an eye while snapping fingers, and so on. After each person has a sound and a movement, have him or her demonstrate them while other group members follow along so that all players will know each other's sound and movement.

3. To play, the first person slaps thighs and says "What's the name of the game?" The rest of the group, also slapping thighs, responds "Thumper!" The leader, still slapping, says "How do you play?" The group, still slapping, answers "You thump!"

4. Immediately after this beginning ritual, the group begins the cadence of slapping thighs twice and then snapping fingers — first the left and then the right hand. While the rest of the group snaps the fingers of the left hand, the leader does his or her own sound and movement. While the group snaps the fingers of the right hand, the leader does the sound and movement of another person in the group. This passes responsibility for carrying on the game to the new person. Everyone slaps thighs. Then the person whose sound and movement the leader has selected repeats his or her own and then does the sound and movement of someone else while the rest of the group snaps fingers. The sound and movement is thus passed around the circle from person to person.

5. If someone fails to recognize his or her own sound and movement the game begins again. The object of the game is to see how long players can keep it up before making a mistake.

CONDUCTING

A conductor leading an orchestra uses a form of sign language in order to communicate ideas to musicians. This game requires a similar type of nonverbal expression.

MATERIALS

None

ROOM ARRANGEMENT

As is

TIME

20 minutes

DIRECTIONS

1. As a group, decide on some simple hand signals that refer to a specific sound. For example, raising a hand in the air might mean a high-pitched "ooh"; making a fist, a deep growl; wiggling a finger, a "boo"; and showing all ten fingers, a shout of "hooray!"

2. Begin with four simple sounds and signals. Practice them with the group, so that when the signal is given, everyone recognizes it immediately and makes the sound. Do this rapidly, changing the order of the sound signals each time.

3. After everyone has tried each sound a few times, divide players into four groups — one for each sound.

4. Conduct the group using several signals at once so that two or three groups will be making sounds simultaneously. Add a gesture that will suggest loudness and softness. For example, raise one hand to produce a sound. Slowly lower the hand to soften the sound.

5. As the group begins to follow directions and signals with more accuracy, add signals and sounds.

SOUNDINGS

Despite the fact that we talk all the time, few of us have explored the incredible variations that are possible with our voices.

MATERIALS

None

ROOM ARRANGEMENT

Open space

TIME

20 minutes

DIRECTIONS

1. Players sit in a circle and clear throats ready for action. The object of this activity is to see how many different sounds can be made with just voices.

2. Players take turns saying their names as quickly and as slowly as they can, adding voice variations. Players can come up with some remarkable sounds if they draw out the pronunciation of their names for fifteen or twenty seconds.

3. Players close eyes. Start by making a sound — tongue click, hum, beep, whistle, or whatever — and passing it along. The sound is passed from player to player as quickly as possible. Try passing several different sounds at the same time.

4. Open eyes and ask players to imitate a sound — birds in the forest, waves breaking on the beach, traffic sounds, musical instruments, and so forth. Ask players if anyone has a special sound he or she would like the group to guess.

5. Have small groups of players sing the tunes (but not the words) to familiar songs using not their singing voices, but unusual sounds. How would three frogs sound singing the tune to "Row, Row, Row Your Boat"?

CREATING SILENCE

Although this game has a sound foundation, it is actually about silence. Sound and silence, just like other opposites, need each other in order to be understood and appreciated. Players might think they are playing only with sounds, but they are also playing with the absence of it.

MATERIALS

None

ROOM ARRANGEMENT

Open space

TIME

10 minutes

DIRECTIONS

1. Everyone sits quietly in a circle. You begin by making two sounds, "beep — hum," leaving a short silence between. Ask players what they heard. They will probably answer "beep hum" without recognizing the silence. Try again, leaving a longer gap of silence. Explain that silence separates and defines the two sounds just as the two sounds define or "frame" the silence.

2. To demonstrate, have the group hum one continuous sound for thirty seconds. The sound was defined by the silence before and after. Have everyone hum again for thirty seconds, but this time break it with a short silence every ten seconds. Try adding a few more silences to the thirty-second hum to create a rhythm. Keep adding silences until the sound almost disappears.

3. Have everyone close his or her eyes and be as silent as possible. Instruct players to add a sound to the silence, slowly filling it up. Players make random sounds with their voices — beeps, hums, whistles, clicks, and so forth — in order to change the shape of the silence. When the silence becomes filled with an assortment of sounds, reverse the process, slowly emptying the sounds to perfect silence.

SYLLABLE SYMPHONY

Here's an auditory puzzle that takes a good ear to piece together.

MATERIALS

None

ROOM ARRANGEMENT

Open space

TIME

10 minutes

DIRECTIONS

1. Everyone sits in a circle. One person is chosen to be It and goes out of the room.

2. The rest of the group picks one word with three or more syllables, such as the word *De-cem-ber*.

3. Count off by syllables so each person has part of the word — the first person would be *de;* the second person, *cem;* the third, *ber;* the fourth, *de* again; and so on.

4. Pick a song with a simple melody such as "Row, Row, Row Your Boat" or "Yankee Doodle." Each person sings his or her syllable to the tune of the song. For example, one would sing "de, de, de, de," another would sing "cem, cem, cem, cem," and the rest "ber, ber, ber, ber," all together to the same melody.

5. The person who is It comes back into the room. He or she must listen carefully as the group is singing and try to piece together the word.

THE MINISTER'S CAT

The human qualities of cats have always
fascinated people. Although the origin of this
game is not certain, it was no doubt inspired by a
rather colorful feline.

MATERIALS

None

ROOM ARRANGEMENT

Open space

TIME

10 minutes

DIRECTIONS

1. This game is fun if everyone is seated in a circle on the floor. The
object of the game is to provide adjectives describing the minister's cat.
Each new adjective must begin with a different letter of the alphabet. The
first person might say "The minister's cat is an angry cat." The next person
would have to use a word that starts with B and might say "The minister's
cat is a beautiful cat," and so on.

2. It is helpful, and lots more fun, if players tap out a soft rhythm on their
knees throughout the game. Each person should be prepared with a new
word when his or her turn comes, so the rhythm is not broken. The rhythm
emphasizes different parts of the sentence: "The MIN-ister's CAT is a
CRANK-y CAT."

VARIATION

- Try using only adjectives that begin with a particular letter.
- Speed up or slow down the rhythm, depending on how well the group
  is doing.

JAMACKWACK

In the darkest regions of Wackidonia lives the little-known Jamackwack bird. The Jamackwack bird cannot see or fly and prefers to walk backward! As you can probably guess, this is a unique bird, seen only on the rarest occasions — except when playing this game.

MATERIALS

None

ROOM ARRANGEMENT

Open space

TIME

15 minutes

DIRECTIONS

1. Divide the group into two teams. One team will impersonate the famous Jamackwack birds. Since the Jamackwacks only walk in reverse, each player must bend over, hold onto ankles, close eyes, and walk backward. The other team creates a corral by standing hand in hand in a circle around the birds so they can't escape. But there is an open gate, a place where two players do not hold hands.

2. The Jamackwacks must try to find the opening in order to get out. When a Jamackwack discovers the opening he or she starts to yell "Wack! Wack! Wack!" to the other Jamackwacks. The other Jamackwacks, hearing the calls, know where the opening is, and begin to find their way to the gate by following the yells.

3. Meanwhile, the people in the circle around the birds can do nothing to stop their escape except drown out the calls of the free Jamackwack by singing a song ("Old MacDonald," "Row, Row, Row Your Boat," or whatever) as loudly as possible. The more birds that escape, the louder everyone has to sing.

4. When every Jamackwack has finally found the way out of the pen, the birds and the circle switch roles. There are no winners or losers in this game, but it is very amusing to observe how the rarely seen Jamackwacks behave.

ZINK VORTEX

Named after Thomas Zink, infamous player and inventor of fun, the Zink Vortex is an elegant exercise in loco motion.

MATERIALS

None

ROOM ARRANGEMENT

Open space

TIME

5 to 10 minutes

DIRECTIONS

   1. Pick a song to sing while playing this game. Choose a standard that everyone knows such as "Row, Row, Row Your Boat," "The Farmer in the Dell," or "Yankee Doodle" — something that can be performed with gusto.
   2. Join the players in holding hands in a circle.
   3. Release your left hand and begin to coil inward, slowly leading the players on your right hand in a spiral inside the circle.
   4. When you reach the center of the circle, turn around and begin to lead players in a reverse spiral. Players following the incoming spiral will pass outgoing players walking in the opposite direction.
   5. To end, the entire group reforms into a circle and finishes the song.

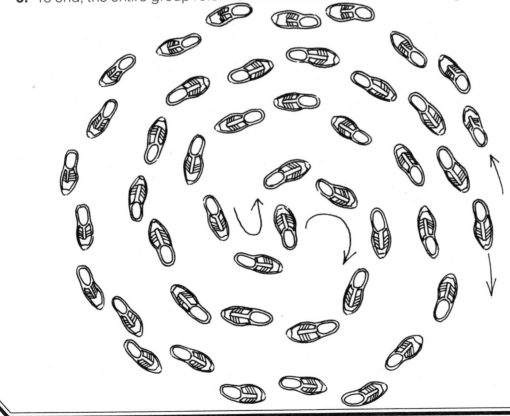

Mind Games

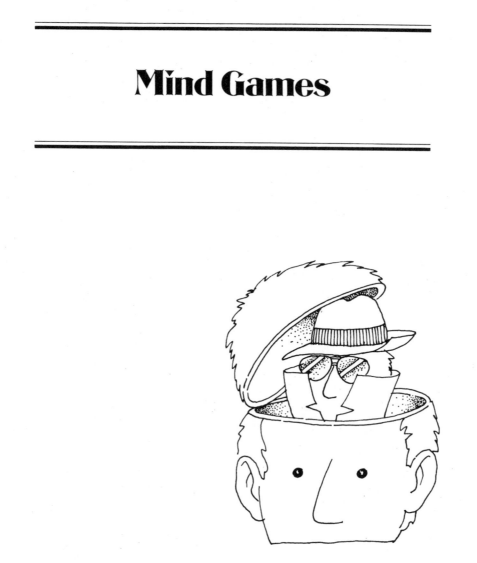

NO, NO, NO!

In this game, everyone agrees to change a sentence just a bit, until it makes little or no sense at all. Rather than making things clearer, each player gets a turn to make things more ridiculous in a more authoritative way.

MATERIALS

None

ROOM ARRANGEMENT

As is or open space

TIME

15 minutes

DIRECTIONS

1. Players can be seated in chairs or in a circle on the floor. The object of the game is to pass a sentence around from person to person, changing one word each time.

2. To play, the first person begins with a simple sentence. For example, "The dog went to sleep." The next person responds in an outraged tone "No, no, no! The hippo went to sleep," changing only one word. The next person might say "No, no, no! The hippo went to Pittsburgh." And so on.

3. Allow only a few seconds for thought. Have a time limit. If someone gets stuck, go on to the next person. Encourage the most unusual word combinations — and don't worry if they don't make sense.

BECAUSE

This game is for those who think they know all the answers.

MATERIALS

None

ROOM ARRANGEMENT

As is or open space

TIME

15 minutes

DIRECTIONS

　1.　Players can be seated as is or on the floor in a circle with their legs crossed. The first player must describe an everyday situation in a simple way. For example, "My shoes are muddy."

　2.　The next person must tell the reason why. For example, "Because it's raining outside."

　3.　The third player must figure out a probable effect. For example, "And my footprints are all over the floor."

　4.　The next player begins again with a simple description and the game follows with the next two responses. Encourage players to state cause and effect rapidly and not to worry about coming up with the best answer. The key is spontaneity.

SOMETHING BAD ABOUT SOMETHING GOOD

In this game everyone will investigate the bad qualities of some very nice things.

MATERIALS

None

ROOM ARRANGEMENT

As is

TIME

25 minutes

DIRECTIONS

1. Ask everyone to think about a favorite thing. It could be a person, a place, or an object.

2. Now have everyone think of its bad qualities. What are the things it cannot do? What are its limitations?

3. Give each person a turn to describe a favorite thing in unfavorable terms without telling the group what the thing is. Encourage players to make their things sound as awful as they can without lying. For example, if the thing is a balloon a player might say "You can't sit on it. You have to be careful that it does not explode. It doesn't last long, and it is impossible to keep in a room full of porcupines."

4. If everyone is stumped and the player has run out of bad things, suggest giving one "good" clue. The first person to guess what it is gets the next chance to describe something. Try, however, to give everyone at least one turn.

VARIATION

This game can be played in reverse by describing the good parts of bad things.

ALPHABET TRAVELS

The more we learn to enjoy using words to express ourselves, the more we are motivated to acquire skills that will help us use language in a variety of ways. This alliteration game should be played for the pure pleasure of playing.

MATERIALS

None

ROOM ARRANGEMENT

Chairs in a circle or open space

TIME

15 minutes

DIRECTIONS

1. Players can be seated in chairs or on the floor in a circle. The object of the game is to go through the entire alphabet, each player making a sentence using as many words as possible with a particular letter. It is helpful to give each player a letter beforehand so everyone has time to prepare. For fairness, leave out the letter X.

2. Each sentence must start with "I am going to . . ." and then name a place and a reason. For example:

- First player: "I am going to Alabama to avoid angry alligators."
- Second player: "I am going to Brazil to balance bright blue bananas."
- Third player: "I am going to Canada to cook colossal cucumbers."
- Fourth player: "I am going to Detroit to demand delicious dinners."
- Fifth player: "I am going to Egypt to enchant elegant elephants."

YES-NO-BLACK-AND-BLUE TABOO

Certain words are unavoidable and we say them so frequently that it's difficult to imagine how we would manage without them. Since practice makes perfect, try avoiding the few words in the name of this game as a beginning.

MATERIALS
None

ROOM ARRANGEMENT
Open space

TIME
15 minutes

DIRECTIONS

1. Divide the room in half with an imaginary boundary line. Separate the group into three teams, each standing in line — one player behind the other — on one side of the boundary line.

2. Explain that you are going to take turns asking players questions and that each player called upon must answer immediately — without hesitation. However, players may not use the words *yes, no, black,* or *blue* in their answers or they will lose their turns and go to the end of the line. Players will soon discover that *maybe* is a good answer and you may have to eliminate that word too. Players who answer successfully are allowed to cross the boundary line.

3. In order to play fast enough to confuse players, prepare a list of questions beforehand. For example:

- "Are you eight years old?"
- "Do you like homework?"
- "What color is a bluejay?"
- "Do you have red pajamas?"
- "Can you ride a bike?"
- "Do you have twenty toes?"
- "What color is a blackboard?"
- "Is your hair green?"

4. Go from team to team asking questions. As more and more players find ways to answer the questions without using the taboo words, they may join teammates on the other side of the boundary line. The first team to get all its players across is the winner.

SECRET WORD

In this game players must watch their language. The group tries to trick a player into saying a secret word before that player guesses it.

MATERIALS

None

ROOM ARRANGEMENT

As is

TIME

15 minutes

DIRECTIONS

1. One person, selected to be It, leaves the room.
2. The rest of the players must agree on a secret word. The word should be a familiar noun or verb used in everyday language, such as *pencil, ruler, map, walk, drink, go,* and so on.
3. After the secret word is selected, the person who is It returns to the room. The rest of the players have five minutes to ask It questions, trying to make him or her answer using the secret word. For example, if the secret word is *eraser,* a question might be "How did you correct the mistakes on your homework?" The players should try to make It use the word as often as possible within the time period. One player should keep track of how many times the secret word is used unknowingly.
4. Meanwhile, It must try to figure out the secret word from the questions, then avoid saying the word until the end of the period. A clever player will try to identify obvious pressure from the group to say a particular word. The group must ask general questions that don't give the word away directly.

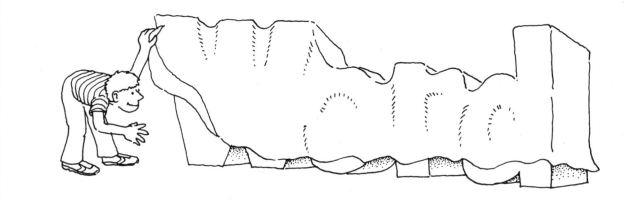

NAME SIX

Naming six objects that begin with the same letter is harder than it seems, especially when there is a time limit.

MATERIALS

A key, an eraser, a beanbag, or any other small object

ROOM ARRANGEMENT

Open space

TIME

15 minutes

DIRECTIONS

1. All players sit in a circle. One player stands in the center.
2. The center player closes his or her eyes while the others pass a small object around the circle. When the center player claps hands, the player caught with the object must keep it. The center person opens his or her eyes and gives the person with the object a letter of the alphabet.
3. The player with the object starts it passing around the circle again, meanwhile naming six objects that begin with the letter named. The six objects must be named before the object makes it around the circle.
4. If the player does not succeed in naming six objects by the time the object is passed around, the player must change places with the one in the center. If he or she names six objects successfully, the game continues with the same player in the center.

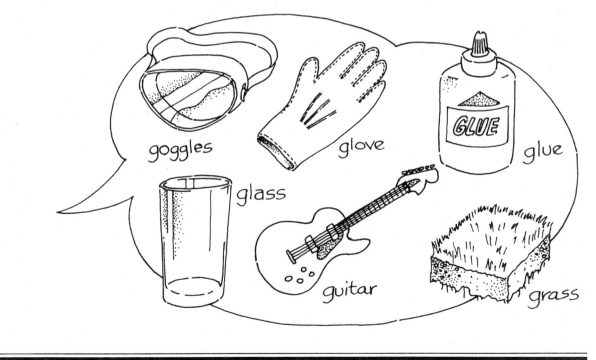

GOING BLANK

Sometimes games can be used to develop our minds in an enjoyable way. Going Blank is a game that people will want to play again and again to test their memories.

MATERIALS

None

ROOM ARRANGEMENT

Open space

TIME

15 minutes

DIRECTIONS

 1. One person is chosen to be It. The entire group agrees upon three categories. Categories can be anything at all — foods, fruits, cities, shoes, TV stars, singers, flowers, birds, and so forth. For the sake of example, let's choose shoes, flowers, and birds.

 2. The group stands in a circle. The person who is It stands in the center, points to anyone in the circle, and names a category: "Shoes!" The person picked must answer within three seconds by naming a kind of shoe: "Loafers!" If the person picked fails to respond or responds incorrectly, that person and the one who is It switch places.

 3. Next the person who is It points to someone across the circle and says "Flowers!" This player responds quickly and says "Daisies!" Next the person who is it might call the first person again and say "Birds!" This might catch the person so off guard that he or she cannot even think of a robin.

 4. As the game continues, the person who is It must keep moving quickly around the circle. One strategy is to hit the same person several times with the same category.

A WHAT?

When is a key not a key? When it's a bibble! In this game, common objects help to create some uncommonly enjoyable confusion.

MATERIALS

2 small common objects (a key, a glove, a pen, and so forth)

ROOM ARRANGEMENT

Open space

TIME

15 minutes

DIRECTIONS

1. Players sit in a circle on the floor with their legs crossed. The object of the game is to pass two objects around the circle in opposite directions.
2. The leader gives each of the two small objects — perhaps a key and a glove — an imaginary name: "froin" and "bibble." The leader offers one object to the player on the right and says "This is a froin." The player to whom it is offered asks "A what?" The leader replies "A froin," and the object is passed. The leader repeats the same ritual with the "bibble" and the player on the left.
3. Both players on the right and left continue the ritual, with one exception. When the next player asks "A what?" the person offering the object turns back to the previous passer and asks "A what?" The "A what?" is passed along back to the leader who tells the name which is passed back down the line.
4. At some point in the middle the two objects are going to cross paths. This all will appear chaotic, but hang on and keep going.
5. The game ends when the objects find their way back to the leader.

AS A RULE

Although rules give structure to games we play, most rules are invisible. The following rules structure a game about finding the rules.

MATERIALS

None

ROOM ARRANGEMENT

Open space

TIME

15 minutes

DIRECTIONS

1. Everyone sits on the floor in a circle. One person selected to be It leaves the room.

2. The players remaining in the room choose a rule to use while answering questions. The rule can be hard or simple depending on those playing. For example:

   - Answer questions as if you were the person to your right.
   - All boys make up stories. All girls tell the truth.
   - Each answer must begin with the letter of the alphabet following the letter with which the previous answer began.
   - Players must scratch heads or yawn before answering.
   - Players must answer as if they were their grandparents.
   - Players must answer as if they were an animal.

3. When the person who is It comes back, he or she must find out the rule by asking players questions about themselves. The person trying to guess the rule is allowed to take as long as he or she needs. If it takes too long, players can help by exaggerating the response the rule calls for.

UNDERCOVER LEADER

This popular game challenges the perception of the person who is It and requires all players to act carefully so as not to give away a secret leader's identity.

MATERIALS

None

ROOM ARRANGEMENT

Open space

TIME

10 minutes

DIRECTIONS

1. Players sit in a circle. One player is chosen to be It and sent from the room. Another player is selected to be the undercover leader.

2. The leader begins a movement, such as head nodding, arm moving, or foot tapping, while the rest of the group follows. Explain to the group that they must be careful not to blow the leader's cover by looking at him or her directly.

3. The person who is It comes back into the room and stands in the center of the circle. All those in the circle perform the movements the leader begins. When the leader changes a movement, everyone follows. The person who is It must observe very carefully in order to discover the leader.

4. When the leader is discovered, two other players become It and the new undercover leader.

NOW YOU SEE THEM, NOW YOU DON'T

Our eyes often deceive us and what we think we saw is not always actually what we saw. This game tests our abilities to perceive a situation and remember it exactly.

MATERIALS

None

ROOM ARRANGEMENT

As is

TIME

15 minutes

DIRECTIONS

   1. Six or more players are chosen to leave the room.
   2. Out of sight of the rest of the group, the six players rearrange their clothes — turn jackets inside out, switch ties, wear shoes on their heads, and so forth — and line up one behind the other. When everyone is ready the six players run quickly in and out of the room in a particular formation.
   3. The six players come back into the room out of formation with clothes back in place. The rest of the group must rearrange runners as they appeared when they made their quick entrance and exit.
   4. After the group agrees on the formation and switches they believe they saw, the runners make any necessary corrections.

QUICK CHANGE

Memory can be a very selective thing. Often we seem to recall only the things that interest us. This game tests powers of observation and memory. It's fun to see what we miss in front of our very eyes.

MATERIALS

None

ROOM ARRANGEMENT

Open space

TIME

15 minutes

DIRECTIONS

   1. Each player selects a partner. Both partners face each other observing clothes, hair, accessories, and so on.
   2. Next, partners turn their backs on each other and make three changes in their personal appearance, such as misbuttoning a button, moving a bracelet, unbuckling a belt, and so on.
   3. When both are ready, they turn around and each tries to identify the changes the other has made.
   4. Have players switch partners and make four changes this time. Keep switching partners and adding to the number of changes. Eight changes are usually the most that people can remember.

ANIMALISMS

A mother hen can tell her chicks' peeping from all the other peeping in the barnyard. Will players be able to identify each other by the sounds of their moos?

MATERIALS

A blindfold

ROOM ARRANGEMENT

Open space

TIME

15 minutes

DIRECTIONS

1. Get everyone to stand in a circle. One player, chosen to be It, is blindfolded and stands in the center.
2. When the person who is It says "Go!" the players begin moving around in a circle. When the person who is It says "Stop!" everyone must freeze immediately.
3. The player who is It points in any direction. The person pointed to leaves the circle and stands about a foot in front of the person who is It.
4. The person who is It asks the player to make an animal noise — bark like a dog, moo like a cow, meow like a cat, and so forth. The It must try to guess the player's identity. If he or she succeeds, they change places with each other. If the guess is wrong, the person picked returns to the circle and the one who is It selects a new player.

CLAPPING CLUES

With everyone applauding throughout this game, it's difficult to tell who's losing and who's winning.

MATERIALS

None

ROOM ARRANGEMENT

As is

TIME

15 minutes

DIRECTIONS

   1. One person is selected to go out of the room. The rest of the group picks an object for the person to find.

   2. The person returns to try to find the object while the group claps. As the person gets closer to the object the claps become loud and enthusiastic. If the person gets farther away from the object, the claps become quiet and weak.

   3. When the object is finally found, the person gets a standing ovation!

VARIATION

Have two people go out of the room while the group members pick a movement or gesture the absent two must do together when they return — shake hands, stick out tongues, hop on one foot, and so on. When the partners return, they must try all kinds of activities in order to find the right one. As the partners get closer to doing the activity — for example, if the activity is to shake hands and they are beginning to wave their arms — the applause becomes louder until they hit upon the right gesture. At that moment they get a standing ovation as they bow to the audience while doing their gesture.

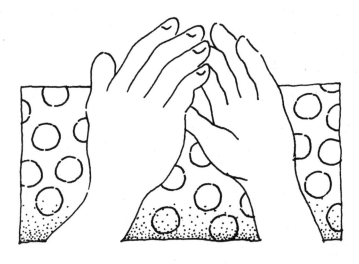

MISSING PERSON

How well does each player know the other people in the group? You'd be surprised how hard it is to recall everyone. This game might be subtitled Forget-Me-Not.

MATERIALS

None

ROOM ARRANGEMENT

As is

TIME

15 minutes

DIRECTIONS

1. Keep the group seated in one area, all visible at one glance.
2. One person, selected to be It, faces away from the group and covers his or her eyes.
3. Another person is selected to leave the room while the rest change their positions.
4. At a signal from you, the person who is It turns around and tries to guess who is missing while the group slowly counts to ten.
5. If the It guesses the one who is missing before the group finishes counting, he or she can have another turn. Otherwise, a new person is selected to be It for the next game.

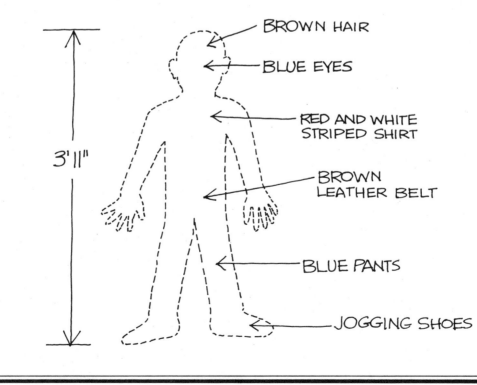

BROWN HAIR

BLUE EYES

RED AND WHITE STRIPED SHIRT

BROWN LEATHER BELT

BLUE PANTS

JOGGING SHOES

3'11"

TRUE DETECTIVE

This version of Hide and Seek might be called Peek and Seek because players must remain in plain sight without being detected.

MATERIALS

None

ROOM ARRANGEMENT

As is

TIME

15 minutes

DIRECTIONS

1. Before the actual game begins have everyone walk around the room in any direction. To prevent the group from being stuck going in only one direction, say "Whenever you see an empty space, move toward that space and fill it. Then keep going, filling other spaces." It is important for everyone to move silently.

2. After a few moments of walking around, give these instructions: "You are each a detective. Select someone in this room to observe. As you walk around the room make sure that you keep that person in sight at all times, but do not let that person know you are watching! Don't be obvious."

3. Let everyone wander around and shadow each other for a few minutes. Remind everyone not to talk.

4. Next, tell players they must try to figure out who is watching them. Have them make it difficult to be seen by dodging in and out of the group. Meanwhile, players have to remember to keep an eye on the person they're observing.

5. To end the activity, say "Follow your person wherever he or she goes." Players will eventually arrange themselves into a line. Ask players if they properly identified their detectives.

CENSORED SEVENS

Censored Sevens is a counting game which seems simple enough — except when it comes to sevens. This game is sometimes called Buzz because the word *buzz* replaces all numbers with seven in them and all multiples of seven.

MATERIALS

None

ROOM ARRANGEMENT

As is

TIME

15 minutes

DIRECTIONS

1. Players stand in a circle ready to count off. Any time a seven shows up — 7, 17, 27, 37, 47, and so forth — or a multiple of seven — 14, 21, 28, 35, 42, 49, and so forth — the number is replaced by the word *buzz*. For example, 1-2-3-4-5-6-Buzz!-8-9-10-11-12-13-Buzz!

2. The object of the game is to get to 100 without making a mistake. If one person forgets to buzz, then everyone has to go back to the beginning and start over.

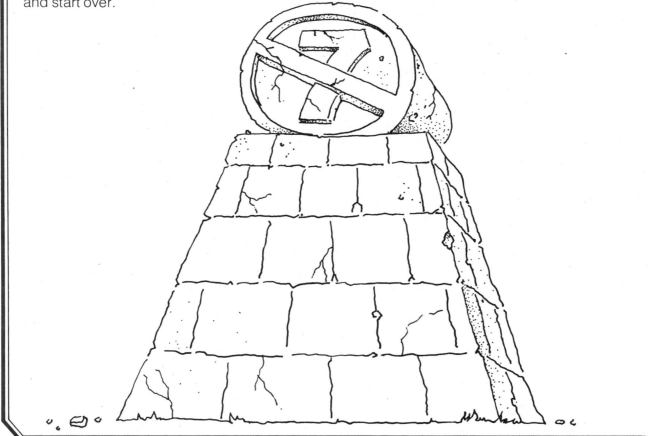

NUMBER, PLEASE

This game helps to increase players' abilities to concentrate and to listen for clues. It works well as a warm-up activity for group play sessions.

MATERIALS

None

ROOM ARRANGEMENT

Chairs in a circle

TIME

15 minutes

DIRECTIONS

1. Players sit in chairs in a circle and count off from one, going clockwise around the room.

2. The game starts when player 1 calls out the number of one of the other players.

3. The person whose number has been called answers by immediately calling out another number. The next person whose number is called continues by calling another number, and so on. Players are not to hesitate when their turns come. When the game is flowing at its best, the number calling can become fast and furious.

4. Eventually, someone will make a mistake, either by not answering at all, by calling his or her own number, or by calling out a number nobody has. That person moves to the last seat and becomes the largest number in the circle. The rest of the group moves counterclockwise up one seat until the seat of the person who made the mistake is filled. For example, 16 is thinking about the day off next week and doesn't answer when that number is called. So 16 moves to the last seat, which is 30. Then 30 moves to 29, 29 moves to 28, 28 to 27, and so on down the line, until number 17 fills 16's seat. The people whose numbers are below 16 do not move. They stay in their seats and keep their numbers.

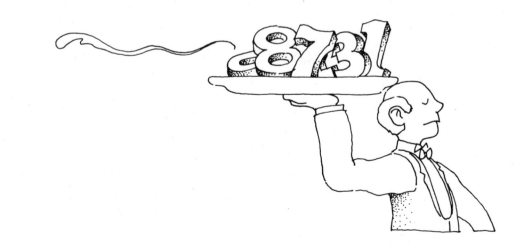

SPELLBOUND

Spellbound is one of those games that could use some magic theatrics, such as a puff of smoke or dramatic gestures. This suspenseful game can be played in a few minutes. The object of the game is to find the person who has the magic touch before you fall under the spell.

MATERIALS
None

ROOM ARRANGEMENT
Open space

TIME
15 minutes

DIRECTIONS
 1. To begin, the Magician must be chosen secretly so no one knows who it is. To do this, have players stand in a circle with eyes closed. One player, also with eyes closed, stands in the center of the circle and asks all players to hold out their thumbs. The person in the center turns around three times, stopping to pick a thumb. The person whose thumb is chosen is the Magician. Players drop their hands to their sides and open their eyes. The identity of the Magician is known to only one!
 2. After the Magician is selected, everyone begins to mill around, shaking hands as if it were a fancy party. The Magician turns his or her victims into "stone" with a gentle magical scratch on the palm while

innocently shaking hands. When a person feels the magic scratch, he or she does not turn into stone immediately, but continues to move around for a few minutes (so as not to give away the Magician's identity). When the spell does take effect, the player slowly turns into stone with appropriate theatrics (gasping for air, moving like a robot, sinking in slow motion to the floor) and then remains as still as possible until the game is over.

3. Those players not turned into stone must find the Magician by catching him or her giving the magic handshake, or by the process of elimination. When a player wants to guess the identify of the Magician, he or she yells, "I reveal!" With hand raised in the air, the player waits for someone to second the revelation. If that doesn't happen, the game continues. If someone does second the revelation, both players stand frozen with hands in the air, count to three, and point together at the suspected Magician. If they point at two different people (even if one *is* the Magician), they continue the game as if nothing had happened. If they they point at the same person but that person is not the Magician, they turn to stone. If they both pick the Magician, they win! The game ends when the Magician is discovered or when everybody is turned to stone.

REINCARNATOR

This is a lively game played with lots of spirit—
from beyond!

MATERIALS

None

ROOM ARRANGEMENT

Open space

TIME

10 minutes

DIRECTIONS

1. Players stand in a circle with arms stretched toward the center. Instruct players to close their eyes. Then say "Thumbs up!" Touch one person's thumb and he or she becomes the Reincarnator. The Reincarnator can transform people into animals simply by whispering "You're a cow" (or horse or bird or hippopotamus or whatever). Other players are allowed to speak, but no other player is allowed to say "You're a . . ." except the Reincarnator.

2. After the Reincarnator is selected, everyone begins to mill about as if at a party. Players greet each other, shake hands, and chat.

3. When the Reincarnator says quietly to another player "You're a turtle," that player should not give the Reincarnator away, but should after a few moments, slowly change into the animal. Gradually players will turn into ducks, cows, chickens, and so forth.

4. If a player thinks he or she knows the identity of the Reincarnator, the player raises a hand and says loudly "I suspect!" The player then points to the suspect and says "You're a fish" (or other animal). If the person accused is indeed the Reincarnator, he or she becomes the animal named. If the accused is *not* the Reincarnator, the accuser becomes the animal and the game continues.

GET IT TOGETHER

People have countless reasons for why they sort and group themselves as they do. In this game, players sort and group themselves and perhaps learn new things about each other in the process.

MATERIALS

None

ROOM ARRANGEMENT

Open space

TIME

20 minutes

DIRECTIONS

1. Players line up in order, according to a direction you give. After the direction is given, players must seek information from each other so as to know how to put themselves in order. Here are some examples of the kinds of directions you might give:

- "Line up according to shoe size, from biggest to smallest."
- "Line up according to birthdays, from January to December."
- "Line up in alphabetical order using your last names. Can you rearrange the group to spell a word using the first letter of each last name?"
- "Line up according to your home address numbers from lowest to highest."

2. Have everyone gather into groups that share certain characteristics. Here are some examples of characteristics you might name:

- "Gather into groups according to the color of your socks."
- "Gather into groups according to the number of brothers and sisters you have."
- "Gather into groups according to your favorite ice cream flavor."
- "Gather into groups according to your favorite TV star."

Action Games

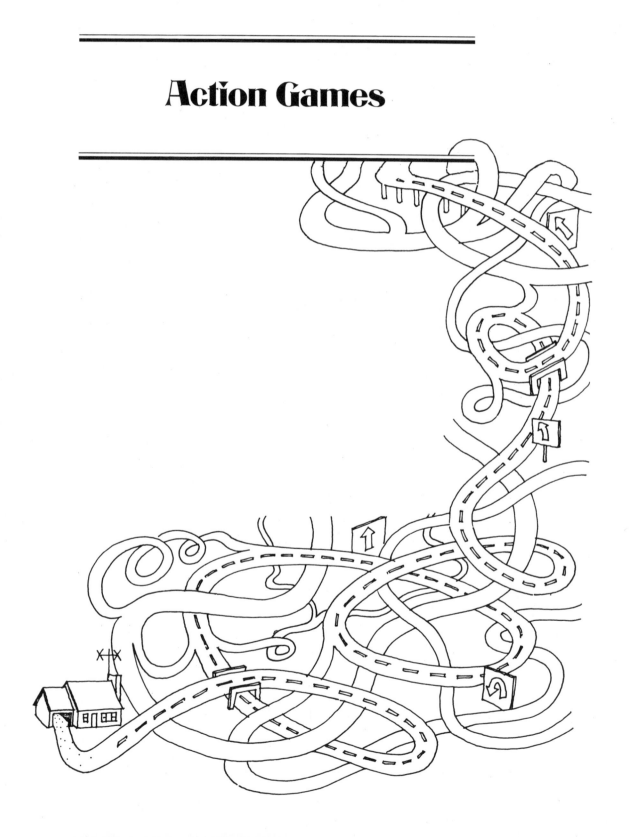

QUICK! LINE UP!

This is a rather active game that needs as much space as possible. It's not a square dance, but you could call it a dancing square.

MATERIALS

None

ROOM ARRANGEMENT

Open space

TIME

15 minutes

DIRECTIONS

1. Arrange the group into a square with an equal number of people on each side. When everyone is in position, stand in the middle.

2. The object of the game is for the people on all four sides of the square to remain in the same position in relationship to the person in the middle. This means that people in front stay in front of the leader, people in back stay in back of the leader, people on the right stay on the right, and people on the left stay on the left. When you move into a new position, the people in the square must move themselves into the same position as before.

3. To begin, make sure everyone knows his or her position. Then, quickly face in a different direction and say "Quick! Line up!" Everyone must move as quickly as possible (without running) to reestablish the square around you. You may turn a lot or a little — one time, a 30-degree turn; next time, a quick 330-degree turn into your original position. There are no winners or losers, just the challenge of being a square.

PERSON TO PERSON

This game helps bring players closer together in some pretty unusual ways.

MATERIALS

None

ROOM ARRANGEMENT

Open space

TIME

15 minutes

DIRECTIONS

1. Each player selects a partner while one person remains free to be the Caller.

2. The Caller names two body parts which the partners must then try to have touch each other. For example, "nose to knee" would have the two partners bent over with their noses touching each other's knees. The contortions can become comically complicated.

3. If the Caller says "person to person," everyone must change partners and the Caller selects a partner also. The person left without a partner after the change becomes the new Caller. If some players are inclined to remain Caller for too long, impose a time limit for each Caller.

NOSE TOES

If we are to have seriousness it is important to have silliness. After all, how could we recognize either if the other didn't exist! This is a silly game — seriously.

MATERIALS

None

ROOM ARRANGEMENT

Open space

TIME

15 minutes

DIRECTIONS

  1. Have players sit in a circle on the floor.

  2. The leader begins by turning to a neighbor and saying "This is my nose" while pointing to his or her toes. The next person repeats "This is my nose" and points to toes, and then adds another silly statement, such as "This is my ear" while pointing to an elbow. The next person repeats the last sentence — "This is my ear" — and the accompanying gesture, and then adds another. This continues around the circle.

  3. To keep a lively pace try having everyone clap in rhythm so that each person will want to move along quickly.

VARIATION

Keep everyone clapping in rhythm. One by one, have each player name two body parts while pointing to the opposite. For example, "This is my ear" (while pointing to the nose), "and this is my nose" (while pointing to an ear). After each turn the entire group repeats the statements without missing a beat.

NEW ODDS

It's amazing how much fun a standard childhood game can be when a few changes make it almost new again. In the traditional game of Odds and Evens, players quickly raise and lower their fists three times before they call out *odd* or *even,* and show one or two fingers. If the total is three fingers the person calling out "odd" is the winner. If two or four fingers are showing the "even" caller is the winner. In case both players make the same call, it's a tie. Although players still like this unadorned version, here's an odd way to make it even more fun.

MATERIALS

None

ROOM ARRANGEMENT

Open space

TIME

10 minutes

DIRECTIONS

   1. Have the players pair up. Practice the traditional game of Odds and Evens several times.
   2. Each pair of players is limited to ten "throws." The loser of a throw must change one element of his or her appearance, such as untie a shoe lace, unbutton a button, turn a jacket inside out, and so on.
   3. If a person whose appearance has been changed *wins* a throw, he or she can change back one element to its original appearance.
   4. At the end of the ten throws, the player with the fewest changes is the winner. Players can switch partners and begin again.

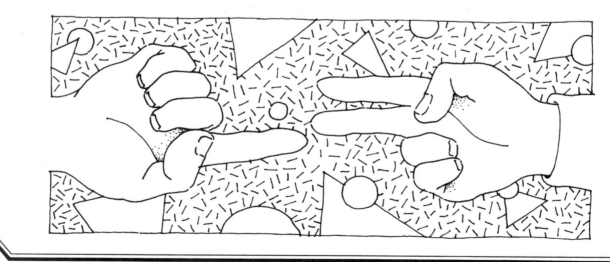

ALL BIRDS FLY

Like Simon Says, this game tries to catch people off guard with the unexpected.

MATERIALS
None

ROOM ARRANGEMENT
Open space

TIME
20 minutes

DIRECTIONS
1. One person is chosen to be It. Standing in front of the class, It says "All birds fly."
2. Next, the one who is It names ten things — birds, animals, or objects — and says they fly. For example, "Eagles fly. Buses fly. Bananas fly. Buildings fly. Robins fly. Rabbits fly. Horses fly. Pigeons fly. Carrots fly. Cookies fly." While reciting the list, It flaps his or her arms.
3. Whenever the player who is It actually names a bird, all players flap their arms. The object of the game is to catch people flapping their arms when the one who is It names something that is not a bird. The player who is It can do this by listing things rapidly or staggering things to confuse the group members and catch them unexpectedly.
4. If players flap when something other than a bird is named, they are out of the game. After the person who is It finishes listing the ten things, a new It is chosen and the players who are out can reenter.

VARIATION
This game can be played with other categories, such as "All fish swim" and "All animals walk."

KUNG THUMB

Those in the group who admire oriental martial arts such as karate or aikido can invest this nonviolent wrestling game with all sorts of kung-foolish drama.

MATERIALS

None

ROOM ARRANGEMENT

Open space

TIME

10 minutes

DIRECTIONS

1. Everyone picks a partner. Partners stand facing each other.
2. Each player closes one hand into a fist (both partners must use the same hand), raises the thumb, and then opens the fist slightly in order to interlock with the partner's hand. Partners should be clasping hands with thumbs upright.
3. The object of the game is for one partner to put the other's thumb down. As in martial arts meets, all sorts of grunts and shouts add drama to these bouts.

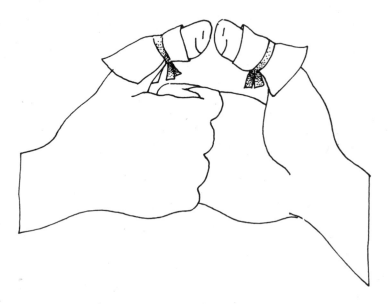

BALANCING ACT

This is a tag game in which players must keep a level head. If players don't stay cool and calm, they may lose their tops.

MATERIALS

2 chalkboard erasers

ROOM ARRANGEMENT

As is

TIME

10 minutes

DIRECTIONS

  1. Players remain in their seats. One person is chosen to be It and is given two chalkboard erasers.
  2. The person who is It puts one eraser on his or her head and walks around the room. When the person who is It puts the second eraser on another player's desk, that player immediately puts the eraser on his or her head and follows the one who is It.
  3. As both players walk, they must balance the erasers on their heads without using hands. Dropping an eraser means stopping to pick it up and replace it, thus losing time.
  4. The second player tries to tag the person who is It before he or she returns to the second player's vacant seat. If the person who is It reaches the seat and sits down, the second player receives the other eraser and becomes the new It.

KNOT ME!

Are the people in your group fit to be tied? This game will help them unwind.

MATERIALS

None

ROOM ARRANGEMENT

Open space

TIME

10 minutes

DIRECTIONS

1. All but two players join hands and form a circle. The two players not in the circle turn away from the circle and close their eyes.

2. The players in the circle twist themselves into a human knot by going over, under, and around arms, legs, and bodies without breaking hands.

3. The players whose backs are turned can open their eyes and try to figure out how to untangle the group. The group must cooperate with the two untanglers as they try to reverse the twisted knot.

IN GEAR

One might call this game a turn on, but it's really an excuse to mesh around.

MATERIALS

None

ROOM ARRANGEMENT

Open space

TIME

10 minutes

DIRECTIONS

1. Divide players into groups of five, seven, nine, and eleven (or comparable numbers).
2. Each group becomes a "gear" by forming a tight circle facing inward and grasping each other's hands.
3. The gears gather together in the center of the room. The smallest gear touches the next largest one, which touches the next largest one, and so on.
4. Each player is a "gear tooth." As gears turn, players in one circle are to fit or mesh into spaces between gear teeth in the adjoining circle.
5. The smallest gear begins turning and starts the others turning. The smaller the gear, the faster it turns. The smallest gear can speed up or slow down, causing the other gears to follow suit.
6. You can add to the fun by reversing the direction by saying "Change!" Players make a screeching sound as they put on the brakes and go into reverse.

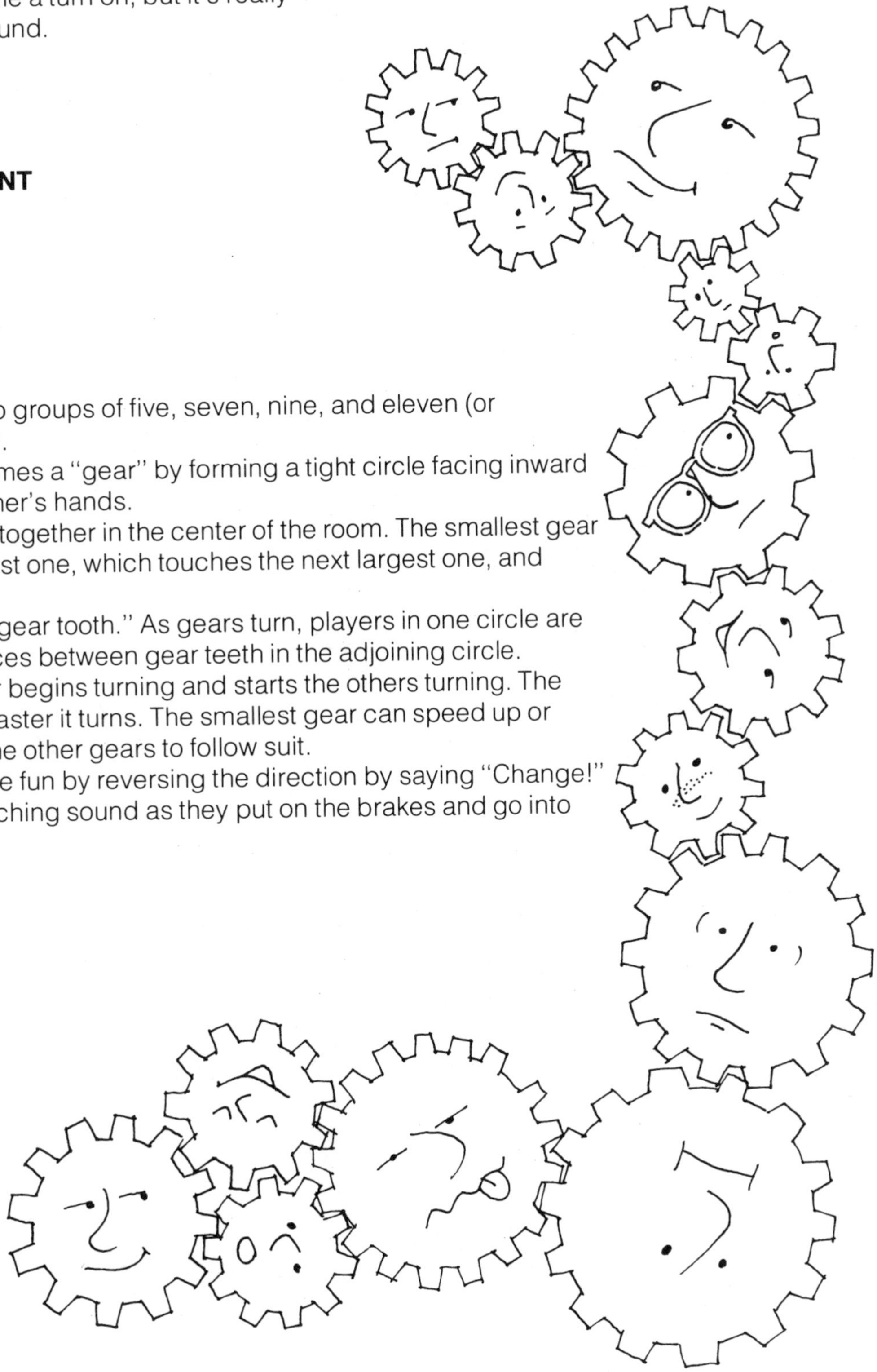

BUBBLING OVER

Here's an air-raising experience. Players will float away, but their feet will remain securely on the floor.

MATERIALS

None

ROOM ARRANGEMENT

Open space

TIME

5 minutes

DIRECTIONS

1. Push furniture to the edges of the room and divide the group into groups of three. "Bubbles" are formed by three players holding hands in a circle.

2. When all the bubbles are ready to take off, they float around the room carefully, not bumping into any other bubbles. Music adds a light touch to this game. Something like a Strauss waltz keeps everyone flying high.

3. Bubbles must try to avoid other bubbles as long as possible. They can spin and twirl gracefully. When bubbles inevitably collide, they pop, then merge into bigger bubbles.

4. As more and more small bubbles pop, the large group bubble continues to grow. At the end, the big bubble sadly faces the fate of all bubbles and collapses with a pop on the floor.

VARIATION

Try this game with eyes closed.

HUMAN MIXMASTER

Here's a confusing game that sorts itself out in a very entertaining way.

MATERIALS

None

ROOM ARRANGEMENT

Open space

TIME

15 minutes

DIRECTIONS

1. Instruct everyone to stand in a circle. The object of the game is simple: simultaneously all players must walk directly across the diameter of the circle and reform into a circle. The circle should be exactly the same as before, but with players facing the opposite direction.

2. After players have done this once or twice, have them keep their hands at their sides and not bump into anyone as they walk. Strategies will start to emerge. Some people will walk slowly while others will walk quickly to get across.

3. If a player does accidentally bump into someone else, he or she must say "beep!" There will probably be quite a few "beeps" as people cross.

4. Finally, everyone must execute the move across the circle with eyes closed.

BRIDGING THE GAP

There are all sorts of bridges, from simple truss to suspension. This game adds a new category: the human bridge!

MATERIALS

None

ROOM ARRANGEMENT

Open space

TIME

15 minutes

DIRECTIONS

  1. This is a single cooperative activity that involves the entire group. The object of the game is to build a human bridge from one end of the room to the other.

  2. Divide the room into two territories with an imaginary valley in between. Explain to the group that everyone must get across the valley in order to escape the terrible ogre who will turn everyone to stone forever! (The story is up to you.) Unfortunately there is no bridge to get across.

  3. After group members are adequately motivated, explain their only hope is the human bridge! The human bridge is sort of an obstacle course made by everyone in the group. One by one, each person adds to the bridge, standing or crouching in position. Each person must climb over or crawl under the players who are already part of the bridge. For example, the first person might stand with his or her legs apart. The second person crawls under the first person and then crouches into a ball. The third person crawls under the first person and over the second person and ends up as a tunnel on all fours. Players might end up in all sorts of positions, holding arms in hoops for others to step through or lying on the floor for others to step over.

  4. This continues as each new player is added. When the last player is added to the bridge, the first player can now crawl through to the other end. This continues until the entire group has moved to the other side and is safely away from the terrible ogre.

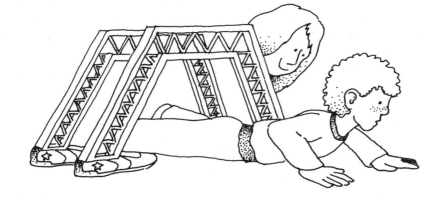

SHOE STEW

Shoe Stew is a tangle of shoes trying to find their mates. The object of the game is to figure out ways to reunite two different shoes at the same time.

MATERIALS
Shoes from all players

ROOM ARRANGEMENT
Open space

TIME
15 minutes

DIRECTIONS

1. All players remove their shoes and put them in a pile in the center of the room.

2. Next, everyone randomly picks two different shoes that are not his or her own.

3. After putting on the two shoes (without buckling or tying), each player tries to locate the matching shoes. When one matching shoe is located, both shoe wearers put their feet next to each other, shoe to shoe. Both players continue to search for the matches to their other shoes. To do this, players will have to twist and hop together. The challenge is to try to figure out how to match both shoes.

4. At the end when shoes are finally reunited, group members will find themselves part of a twisted tangle of arms and legs.

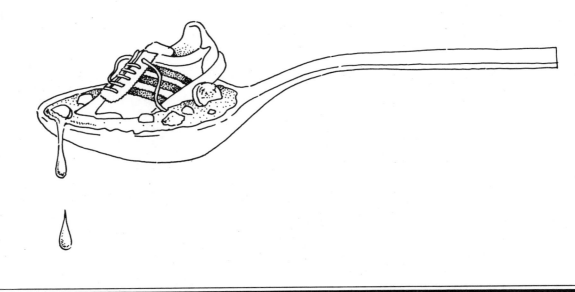

CHEF'S SALAD

Here's a salad that doesn't need oil and vinegar because the only things that get tossed around are the players.

MATERIALS

None

ROOM ARRANGEMENT

Chairs in a circle

TIME

15 minutes

DIRECTIONS

  1. One person is selected to be the Chef. The rest of the group divides into pairs.
  2. Each pair chooses a single vegetable. No two pairs should be the same vegetable. If the group is too large, divide vegetables into groups of four.
  3. Form a circle of chairs with the person who is the Chef standing in the center. People with the same vegetable should avoid sitting close together.
  4. The Chef calls out the name of a vegetable. Those people whose vegetable is called get up and switch chairs quickly while the Chef tries to grab one of the vacant places. The person who was not able to sit down becomes the new Chef while the former Chef becomes the vegetable.
  5. When the Chef calls "Chef's Salad!" everyone changes seats. The player left without a seat is the new Chef.

A safety note: Use sturdy chairs and be sure there is lots of room. If using chairs seems to be too dangerous, have players sit on the floor in a circle.

DOG BONE

Every dog has its good days and its bad days. In this game, every dog has a bone to pick.

MATERIALS

A chalkboard eraser, a beanbag, or any other grabbable object

ROOM ARRANGEMENT

As is

TIME

15 minutes

DIRECTIONS

1. Players remain seated except for one person selected to be the Dog. The Dog sits with eyes closed, facing away from the group. A "bone" — eraser, beanbag, or other object — is placed behind the Dog and in front of the group.

2. Select one player at a time to try to slip up quietly and get the bone. If the Dog hears a sound, he or she barks like a dog and the would-be bone thief returns to his or her seat. If a player is able to take the bone without being heard, the player returns to his or her seat and hides it. The rest of the group then chants "Dog, Dog, where's your bone?"

3. The Dog then turns around and has three chances to guess who has the bone. If the Dog guesses incorrectly, the groups says "No!" If the guess is correct, the group applauds. In both cases, the one who stole the bone becomes the next Dog.

STEAL THE BACON

Steal the Bacon is a traditional favorite. It provides an opportunity to discuss the elements of competition and to emphasize the values of teamwork and developing strategies.

MATERIALS

A beanbag, a ball of yarn, a handkerchief, or any other object easy to pick up

ROOM ARRANGEMENT

Open space

TIME

25 minutes

DIRECTIONS

1. Use masking tape to make two parallel lines twelve feet apart on the floor.

2. Divide players into two teams and have them line up on the taped lines, facing each other. Have the teams count off simultaneously so that players' numbers on one team will match players on the other team.

3. The leader throws the "bacon" (beanbag or whatever) into the center between the two lines and calls out a number. Each of the two players who have that number try to retrieve the bacon and get it back across his or her team line without being tagged by the other player. If a player is tagged before getting across the line, there is no score and the bacon is dropped where the player is tagged. If the player gets the bacon across the line, his or her team gets a point.

VARIATION

To make the game a little more challenging, the leader may call out two numbers. For example, the leader calls out numbers 4 and 7. Players 4 and 7 of one team work together against 4 and 7 of the other team. If 4 grabs the bacon and is tagged, the bacon is dropped immediately and 4 may not try for it again. But 7 can still try to get the bacon and 4 can help by blocking or faking the opponents. If both members of the same side are tagged, the play is over and the bacon is left in its last position on the floor.

SMAUG'S JEWELS

Smaug's Jewels is a version of Steal the Bacon with a mythical twist. In J.R.R. Tolkien's book *The Hobbit*, Smaug is a dragon who protects a treasure of gold and jewels. In this game, the dragon may not be as intimidating and the jewels not as priceless, but it is still a challenge to steal the treasure without getting caught.

MATERIALS

A beanbag, a ball of yarn, a handkerchief, or any other object easy to pick up

ROOM ARRANGEMENT

Open space

TIME

20 minutes

DIRECTIONS

1. One person is chosen to be Smaug and stand guard over the "jewels" (beanbag or whatever). Everyone else forms a circle around Smaug.

2. The group standing around Smaug must try to steal the treasure without being tagged. Those touched by Smaug are frozen in place and can no longer try for the treasure.

3. Smaug must try to defend the treasure. It's always surprising how far loud roars, evil glances, and some fancy footwork will go to ward off invaders. Smaug, if daring, can wander away from the treasure to tag potential thieves.

4. Usually one part of the group will try to tease Smaug away from the loot to help someone from another part of the circle catch the dragon off guard. The thief can try to dive from behind Smaug and get the jewels before being tagged. If the dragon hovers over the treasure there may have to be a mass charge which sacrifices a few players for the sake of the jewels.

TRAFFIC PATTERNS

This game makes rush hour look like a picnic.
These rules of the road may drive everyone crazy
as players make up their own routes and
highways.

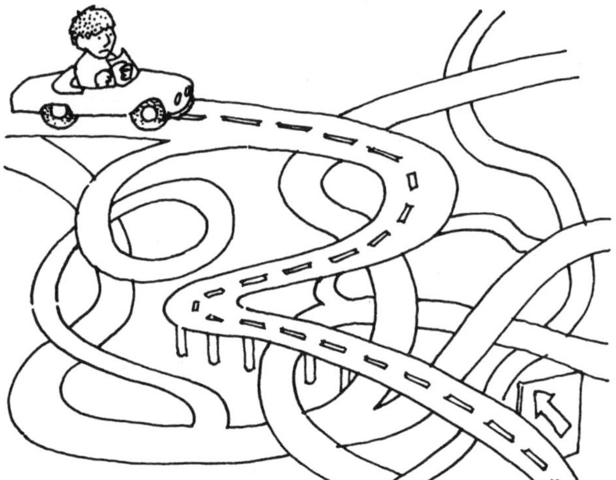

MATERIALS

None

ROOM ARRANGEMENT

Open space

TIME

10 minutes

DIRECTIONS

1. Players divide into pairs — one is a "car" and the other is the "driver."
Cars hold hands out in front (imitating headlights) and close their eyes.
Drivers keep their eyes open and steer cars by standing in back and
placing their hands on their partners' shoulders.

2. One set of a car and a driver is chosen to be It. As in the traditional
game of tag, the person who is It tries to tag another player. In this game,
cars only tag cars. Drivers carefully maneuver cars around other cars
trying to avoid getting tagged. Speeding is not allowed.

3. When the car that is It tags another, the car that was tagged becomes
the new It. Cars and drivers switch roles and the game continues.

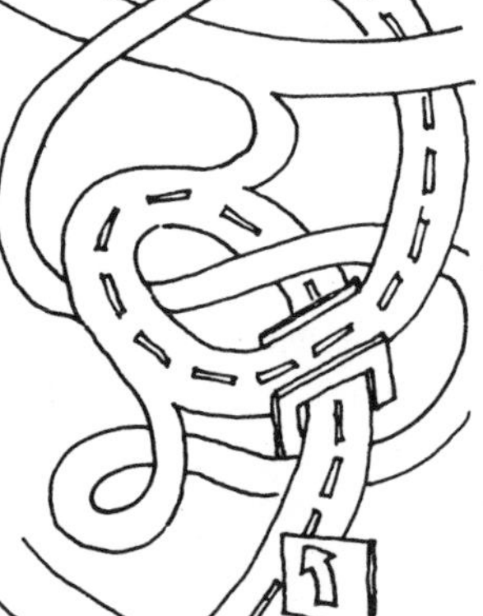

AIRPORT

When large airliners land, they use radar and complicated instruments rather than relying only on the vision of the pilot. In this activity, players rely on senses other than sight.

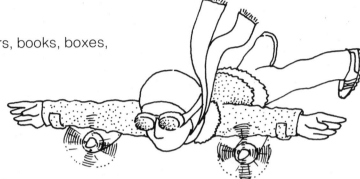

MATERIALS

Objects found in the room (chairs, books, boxes, shoes, and so forth)
A blindfold

ROOM ARRANGEMENT

Open space

TIME

20 minutes

DIRECTIONS

1. Divide the group into pairs. One person becomes the "pilot" while the other partner is the "air traffic controller." One pair runs the course. The rest of the players become the runway by forming two lines about eight feet apart with the lines facing each other.

2. Obstacles, such as chairs, books, boxes, shoes, and so on, are placed on the runway. Be careful not to use objects that will be harmful if stepped on or bumped into.

3. The air traffic controller stands at one end of the runway. The pilot is blindfolded and stands at the opposite end. The controller verbally guides the pilot down the runway so that the pilot avoids obstacles and the people on either side.

VARIATION

Try the same game but have two pilots and two controllers working simultaneously.

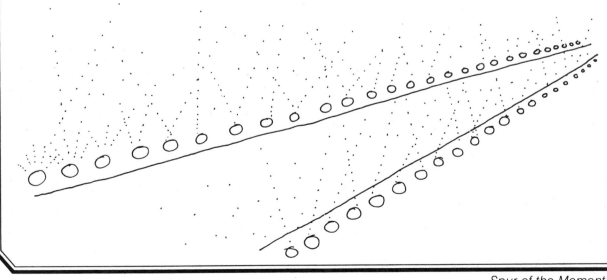

INDOOR TAG GAMES

The objects of tag are always the same — to flee the deadly touch of the person who is It and to remain free. Outdoors, tag is a very active and wide-ranging game. To play it indoors, you must modify the game. The variations here work well in a limited space.

MATERIALS

None

ROOM ARRANGEMENT

Open space

TIME

10 minutes each

DIRECTIONS

Ballet Tag

1. It may seem impossible to keep everyone slowed down in the heat of tagging, but if tag were changed into a dance, like a takeoff on a ballet, the game could become more like theater than battle. To get players in the mood, ask them to demonstrate some slow-motion "ballet" movements, such as gracefully twisting bodies, waving arms, and standing on toes.

2. Introduce music; something outrageously Straussian is fun. Keep the movements very slow. Even if the players hate it, they tend to mock the music with exaggerated movements that add to the game.

Popcorn Tag

1. Games work differently with each group. If Ballet Tag isn't active enough and running is too active, try Popcorn Tag. To begin, all players hop up and down on both feet.

2. When the person who is It tags a player, the two immediately join hands. The two hopping Its set out to tag other helpless hoppers. When other players are tagged they join the hopping chain until there is only one lonely hopper left.

Dog Tag

1. For this game, furniture makes things more challenging. First define boundaries — places players cannot go.

2. Everyone gets down on all fours. In this game, players who are tagged are frozen and can't move until fellow players crawl under them and thaw them out. If the person who is defrosting a frozen player gets tagged in the process, he or she becomes frozen as well. The object of the game is for the one who is It to freeze all players.

Alligator Tag

1. In this version of tag the room is transformed into a swamp and the players become slippery reptiles. Have everyone gather in a circle and lie on stomachs with faces toward the center. The person chosen to be It is in the middle of the circle, also lying on the floor.

2. When It says "Go!" the other alligators must scramble away. Remind players to stay on their stomachs. And please, no biting!

Slow Freeze Tag

1. This is less a competitive game of tag and more a theatrical performance. To begin, divide the group in half — one group to play, the other group to be an audience.

2. Clear as much space in the room as possible, establishing boundaries away from the walls. One person is selected to be it.

3. Players run in slow motion. When It tags another player, the person who is It freezes in position and the tagged person becomes the new It. As more and more people are tagged, the old Its remain frozen in whatever position they were in. The last person to remain unfrozen is the winner.

VARIATIONS

Tag is the perfect game to invent your own variations.

- Have the person who is It try tagging while everyone's eyes are closed.
- Have people who are tagged crawl backward.
- Combine Ballet Tag with Popcorn Tag — players dance until they're tagged, then begin hopping after other players.

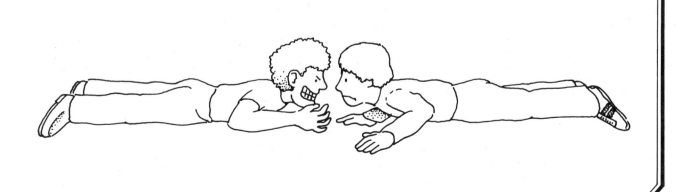

PART TWO
A Little Preparation

Sometimes when you have more time to play, you may want to try some games that require a few special materials and a little more organization. In this section, the activities are still easy to do, but they need certain materials that are not always immediately at hand. You may have to borrow a ball from a gym teacher or buy a stack of file cards from a stationery store. The structure of many of these games is more elaborate and playing time slightly longer than for the games in Part One.

Artful Activities

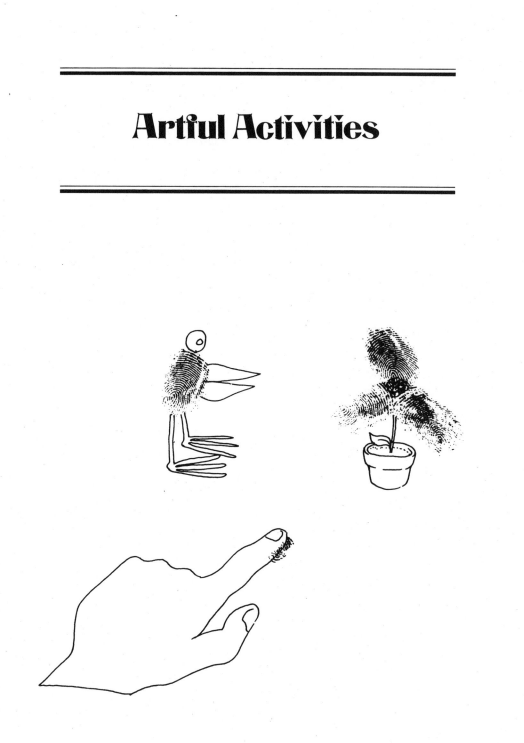

DOT'S DOT

If you've ever completed a dot-to-dot drawing, you realize that there is usually only one solution. In this version, absolutely nobody knows what the picture will be! The only solution is in the imagination of the player.

MATERIALS

A sheet of standard-sized blank paper for each player
A pencil for each player

ROOM ARRANGEMENT

As is

TIME

20 minutes

DIRECTIONS

1. Keep everyone seated in the usual places. Give a sheet of paper and a pencil to each player.

2. Have each player cover the surface of the paper with twenty to thirty dots. Most sure that the dots are large and easy to see. They should be scattered randomly over the paper.

3. Each player passes his or her paper to a neighbor.

4. Tell players to look hard at the dots to see if they can imagine pictures and then connect the dots so that the picture emerges. This isn't as easy as it seems. Sometimes turning the paper in different directions is helpful. Encourage far-out solutions to this perplexing problem.

5. After the dots have been connected and drawings are complete, have each player exhibit his or her drawing.

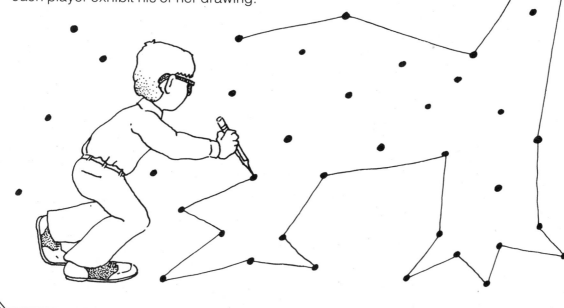

SCRIBBLES

Our imaginations are always working to organize and structure the world, even if no structure exists. We look up at the clouds and see faces take form in their billowy masses. We look down at a crack in the sidewalk and find the shapes of animals and monsters. This activity is another challenge for our ingenuity.

MATERIALS

A sheet of any standard-sized paper for each player
A pencil for each player

ROOM ARRANGEMENT

As is

TIME

20 minutes

DIRECTIONS

1. Keep everyone seated in the usual places. Pass out a sheet of paper and a pencil to each player.
2. The object of this game is to turn the most pointless scribble into something recognizable. Each person draws a simple scribble on the paper and passes it to a neighbor.
3. Now everyone must make this new scribble part of a drawing of a recognizable object or scene.
4. After everyone has finished, have players try to pick out the original scribbles. The one with the most ingeniously disguised scribble gets the Scribble of the Year Award.

RIPPED PUZZLES

What a delight! It's OK to tear the paper!

MATERIALS

A sheet of any standard-sized paper for each
player
A pencil for each player

ROOM ARRANGEMENT

As is

TIME

20 to 30 minutes

DIRECTIONS

   1. Keep everyone seated in the usual places. Pass out a sheet of paper
and a pencil to each player.
   2. Each person must make a drawing, keeping it hidden from the other
players. Have players make their pictures as complicated as they possibly
can, with lots of details covering the entire surface.
   3. When all are finished drawing, have them tear their pictures into an
agreed upon number of pieces; thirty or forty is plenty. The number
depends on the size of the paper, but don't make the pieces unreasonably
small.
   4. Everyone passes his or her puzzle to another player who tries to
reassemble it. The first player to finish gets a ripping round of applause.

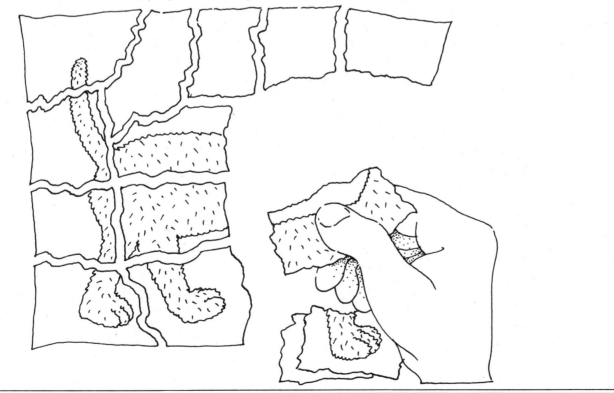

MUTUAL MONSTERS

What would happen if we could switch heads, torsos, and legs with other people? We'd come up with some strange combinations. Prepare yourself because here we go!

MATERIALS

A sheet of any standard-sized paper for each player

A pencil, a crayon, or a felt-tipped marker for each player

ROOM ARRANGEMENT

As is

TIME

20 minutes

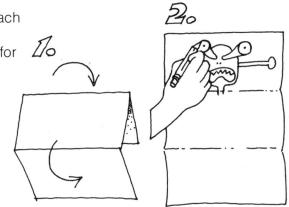

DIRECTIONS

  1. Give each player a piece of paper and a pencil. Have everyone fold the paper into thirds.

  2. On the top third of the paper, each player is to draw the head of a person, an animal, or a made-up creature, continuing the lines of the neck a little bit past the fold. Then players are to fold back the tops so that the pictures are not visible to anyone.

  3. Each person then passes his or her sheet to a neighbor who is to draw a torso and arms in the middle third without looking at the head drawn on the top third. The lines again should be extended slightly beyond the next fold. Once again papers are folded so that the pictures cannot be seen, and then passed along.

  4. The last player connecting the lines adds legs on the bottom third of the paper.

  5. When all players have finished drawing, the sheets are unfolded and shown to the whole group.

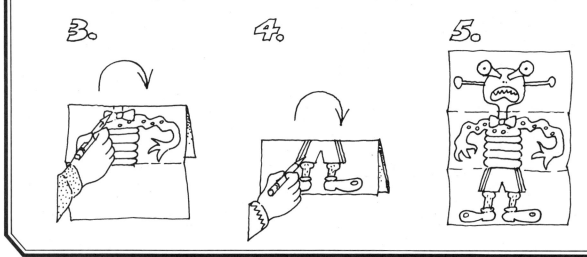

GRAPH-PAPER DRAWINGS

Grid patterns are the basis of a great many designs — everything from newspaper graphics to skyscraper facades to city blocks to checker boards. This activity may uncover some as yet unknown possibilities.

MATERIALS

A sheet of graph paper for each player (the smaller the squares the better)
A pencil or fine-line felt-tipped marker for each player
Assorted crayons

ROOM ARRANGEMENT

As is

TIME

20 to 30 minutes

DIRECTIONS

1. Keep everyone seated in the usual places. Give each player a sheet of graph paper and a pencil or marker.

2. Have everyone conjure up a mental picture of something very common — a flower, an animal, a building, a person. Ask players to think about the details of their pictures — the petals of the flower, the tail on the animal, the windows in the building, and so forth.

3. The task is to draw the picture using the lines of the graph paper. Curves will become a series of small, straight, step-like lines.

4. After the outlines are finished, players can color them with crayons and markers to create texture.

VARIATION

Have everyone think of as many pictures as they can to fill in the small grid squares with tiny drawings.

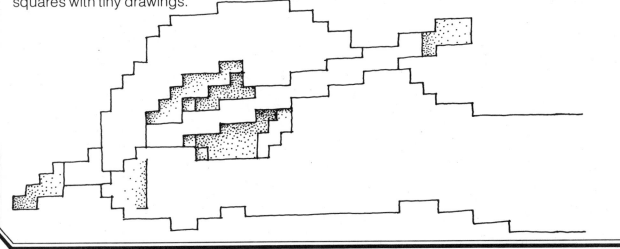

FINGER FESTIVAL

An infant's first toys may be fingers and toes. Why abandon those original playthings? This activity explores some digital delights.

MATERIALS

Watercolors or tempera
A small brush for each player
A cup of water for each group of players
Soap
Towels

ROOM ARRANGEMENT

As is

TIME

25 minutes

DIRECTIONS

1. For this activity arrange players into groups of five or six.
2. Give each group a set of watercolors or tempera and brushes.
3. Have everyone raise the hand he or she does *not* write with. This is the hand that will have the finger puppets.
4. Suggest to players that each finger has a personality of its own. What kind of character could the thumb be? The index finger? How should they be dressed? Should they wear sunglasses, hats, neckties?
5. Everyone can get to work painting faces and clothes on fingers. Players can help each other paint.
6. As the final step, organize a Finger Festival with music and dancing fingers. Suggest that players introduce their fingers to each other and choreograph an all-finger production number. Then have players wash their hands.

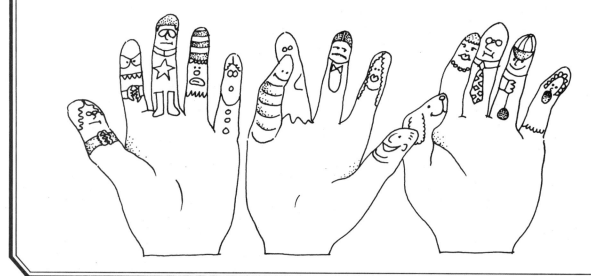

GIVE 'EM A HAND

With a little imagining, players can find hidden
personalities in their hands and can use paints to
help those special traits emerge.

MATERIALS

Watercolors or tempera
A brush for each player
A cup of water for each group of players
Soap
Towels

ROOM ARRANGEMENT

As is

TIME

30 minutes

DIRECTIONS

1. For this activity, arrange players into groups of five or six.
2. Give each group a set of watercolors or tempera and brushes.
3. Have each player raise the hand he or she does not write with. This is
the hand that will be the puppet. Ask players to study their hands to find
the personalities in them. Have them move their hands, wiggle fingers,
make them dance, float like birds, and make fists to see what characters or
creatures start to appear.
4. Everyone can begin to decorate. Players might paint faces on hands,
using fingers for arms, legs, strands of hair, or noses. To get more
elaborate, they can find small pieces of fabric for collars and hats.
5. Organize short, three-minute puppet shows with several characters —
and don't forget to give them a hand at the end before they wash.

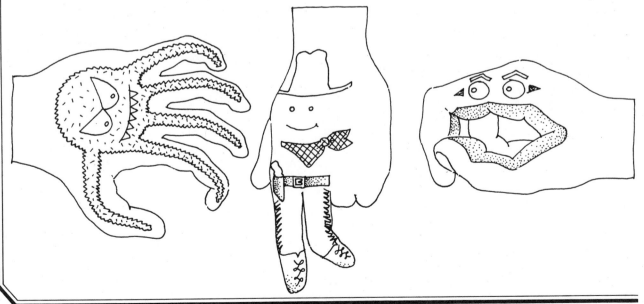

FINGERPRINT PICTURES

We have discovered the individual personalities of our fingers and uncovered the characters of our hands. So what's left? Maybe the question should be what's left and right? The prints of all ten fingers, of course!

MATERIALS

Ink pads
A sheet of paper for each player
Crayons or fine-line felt-tipped markers
Soap
Towels

ROOM ARRANGEMENT

As is

TIME

25 minutes

DIRECTIONS

 1. Divide players into groups of three. Give each person a piece of paper and a crayon or pen. Give each group an ink pad to share.
 2. Ink up fingers by pressing tips into the ink pad.
 3. Players should gently but firmly press their inked fingers on the paper, adding extra pressure with their other hands. It is helpful to experiment with different printing techniques such as rolling fingertips across the paper.
 4. After fingerprints have been printed on the paper, what kinds of things can players make from them? Ask for some suggestions to help get imaginations working.
 5. Everyone can complete fingerprint pictures with pens and crayons. Just a few lines will transform these litle blotches into wonderful beings. Later, players can try printing the sides and heels of their hands to get more complicated forms.
 6. Be careful to remove ink from hands just as soon as the project is finished. Thorough washings with soap and water will be necessary.

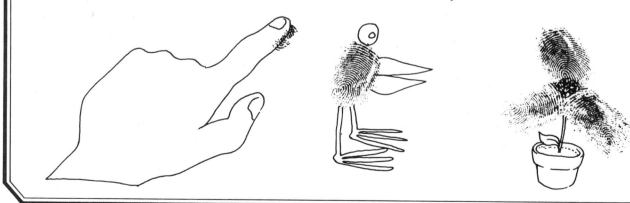

BIG FLIP

Everyone will flip over this instant "movie."

MATERIALS

A 3" x 5" file card for each player
A felt-tipped marker for each player

ROOM ARRANGEMENT

As is

TIME

15 minutes

DIRECTIONS

1. Give each person a file card and a marker.
2. Everyone should agree on a simple basic shape (a circle, a square, a triangle, and so forth) to draw on the cards.
3. Each player should draw the shape, changing its size or position just a tiny bit. For example, if everyone agrees to draw one circle, some can be as large as the edges of the card, while others can be small and placed in various positions on the cards, while still others could be slightly distorted with little bulges or indentations.
4. Collect the cards and try to arrange them so the shapes seem to progress from card to card.
5. Neatly stack cards in a pile, holding them tightly on one end, and flip! The faster the cards are flipped, the more the shape will appear to dance and wiggle all over.

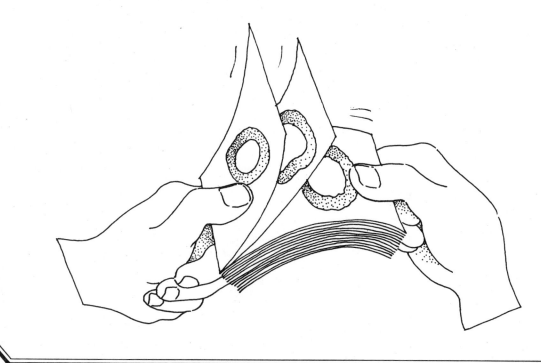

LITTLE FLIPPER

Still pictures can move in a flash with this compact movie studio.

MATERIALS

2 sheets of 3″ x 5″ paper (transparent enough for tracing) for each player
A pencil for each player

ROOM ARRANGEMENT

As is

TIME

10 minutes

DIRECTIONS

1. Pass out two sheets of 3″ x 5″ paper and a pencil to each player.
2. Have players think of a repetitive movement, such as a carpenter hammering a nail, two people shaking hands, or someone waving good-bye.
3. Players draw one picture depicting that movement on one of the two sheets. Then on the other sheet of paper, they trace the first picture, but change slightly the position of head, arms, feet, or whatever part is supposed to be moving.
4. Next, players take one of the sheets and roll it up around a pencil so that it curls. Place the curled picture on top of the flat one. Move the pencil back and forth rapidly to flip the picture and watch it move.

 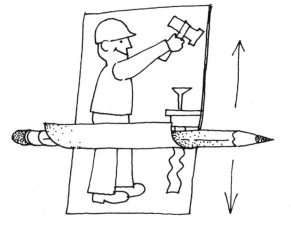

PAPER ORNAMENTS

The most versatile material readily available is paper. A sheet of paper is flexible; yet when folded properly, it can support a brick. In this activity, students explore paper possibilities and at the same time decorate the classroom.

MATERIALS

200 to 300 sheets of paper (construction paper, mimeograph rejects, and so forth)
Scissors for each player
Hole punchers
Staplers
Medium-weight string
Crayons and felt-tipped markers (optional, for additional decoration)

ROOM ARRANGEMENT

As is

TIME

35 to 45 minutes

DIRECTIONS

1. Divide the players into groups of four or five. Give each group a stack of paper, scissors, a stapler, and a hole puncher.

2. There are many different techniques for making paper ornaments, but for this activity encourage players to experiment with inventing their own shapes. To help players get started, demonstrate some of the basic things that can be done with paper. For example:

- rolling — curling into a cylinder
- twisting — bending into a form
- pleating — folding into a repeated pattern
- folding — randomly creasing into free forms
- cutting — slicing into shapes and fringes
- crumpling — crushing and flattening into a textured surface
- tearing — ripping into natural forms
- scoring — pressing a line into the surface to make clean folds
- punching — poking out surface designs and textures

3. Each player takes several pieces of paper and begins to experiment using one or more of these techniques. Paper designs do not have to represent anything. Allow players to cut, twist, and punch their way to creativity. For an added challenge see who can cut the longest continuous ribbon from a single sheet of paper, punch the most holes to make a lacy design, or create the largest paper decoration.

4. Tie a piece of string across the room for a paper ornament display. How many paper ornaments would it take to cover the entire ceiling? Paper ornaments can be used in conjunction with other activities such as paper costumes and puppets (Body Coverings, page 102; Invasion of the Paper-Bag Puppets, page 105).

BODY COVERINGS

Making costumes can be done quickly with this basic body covering. Additions can be added instantly, making the costume any creature imaginable.

MATERIALS

Roll of brown paper 36 inches wide
Scissors for each player
Tape
Staplers
Crayons or felt-tipped markers

ROOM ARRANGEMENT

Open space

TIME

20 minutes

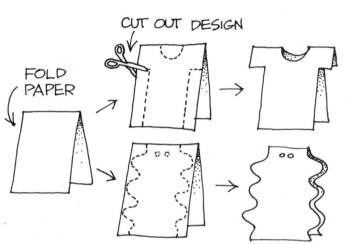

FOLD PAPER

CUT OUT DESIGN

DIRECTIONS

1. Roll out brown paper across the floor. Cut a strip four or five feet long for each person.

2. Have everyone fold his or her strip in half. Folded strips can be cut into various shapes:

- Cut a half circle from the folded edge to make a poncho-type covering.
- Cut the edges of the paper into a shape that fits around head and arms.
- Cut out a space for the face and cut a whimsical design around the edges.
- Create a blob shape or cut a fringe along the bottom.

3. Staple edges around the head and arms, leaving enough extra room for movement.

4. Add paper decorations with tape or stapler (see Paper Ornaments, page 101). Draw designs directly on the costume with crayons or felt-tipped markers.

5. Although it's not absolutely necessary, it's a good idea to have a mirror so that players can see themselves transformed. Organize a costume fashion show and have each player parade through the room. Add a little music and clapping in rhythm and you have the makings of an old-time jig.

STAPLE EDGES

ADD PAPER DECORATIONS

NOSE MASKS

Masks provide instant identities and, in this case, instant expressions. The eyes don't have it, the nose do — er, does.

MATERIALS

A sheet of 5½" x 8½" paper for each player (cut pieces of 8½" x 11" paper in half)
Crayons or felt-tipped markers
Scissors

ROOM ARRANGEMENT

As is

TIME

20 minutes

FOLD

CUT HOLE
FOR NOSE

DIRECTIONS

1. Players are seated at desks or tables. Give each player a piece of paper and a crayon or marker.
2. Players fold their sheets of paper in half and cut a hole for the nose from the folded edge. Since noses are smaller than one may think, start by having everyone cut a small triangular shape from the folded edge. When unfolded, it becomes twice as large so it is better to start small and trim away later.
3. After nose holes have been adjusted, have players put the papers on their noses. When all masks are securely fixed, tell everyone to search for their eyes and carefully mark eye locations with a crayon. Next take off masks and poke a tiny hole for each eye.
4. Decorate masks with faces and expressions. Draw a mouth and two eyes (or three eyes for that matter). Suggest some characteristics — a grouchy frown, a wink, a smile, or even an imaginary face.
5. After masks are finished, everyone can put on an instant expression — ready to face the next assignment.

UNFOLD AND
DRAW A FACE

PLACE
ON
NOSE

INTERGALACTIC PAPER-BAG MASKS

Every child who has grown up in this world of supermarkets has probably made a mask from a grocery bag. Now this simple activity can turn an everyday brown bag into the stuff of science fiction.

MATERIALS

A brown paper grocery bag for each player
Scissors
Assorted colored felt-tipped markers
Masking tape
White glue
Paper scraps, wallpaper books, aluminum
    foil, and other leftover materials

ROOM ARRANGEMENT

As is

TIME

40 minutes

DIRECTIONS

  1. Give each player a grocery bag. Players can share scissors, felt-tipped markers, tape, glue, and scrap materials.
  2. Introduce this activity as something out of this world. Tell players that masks should represent beings from another word or galaxy. Each player must make up his or her own creature, give it a name (Venox, Zipnoid, whatever), and try to imagine its biography — where it lives, what it does for a living, what it eats, and so forth.
  3. To construct masks, have players put bags over their heads and find eye positions. You may have to trim the bottom of the bag so it rests comfortably on small shoulders. Mark eye locations with felt-tipped markers. Remove bags and punch eyeholes with the tips of scissors.
  4. To decorate masks, players can cut pieces of paper and foil to create fantasy eyes, noses, and ears. Paper can be fringed, torn, twisted, and folded into shapes that can be applied to the surface of the bag.
  5. When masks are completed, organize an intergalactic convention of spaced-out creatures to meet, exchange names, and share cultural differences.

ADD PAPER SHAPES AND FOIL

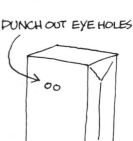

PUNCH OUT EYE HOLES

TRIM TO REST ON SHOULDERS

INVASION OF THE PAPER-BAG PUPPETS

Don't just think of this as another old activity.
Prepare yourself for a puppetulation explosion.

MATERIALS

A paper bag for each player (lunch bag size)
Assorted colored paper
Paper plates
Yarn, buttons, fabric scraps, foil, and other
   leftover materials
Scissors
Masking tape or cellophane tape
White glue

ROOM ARRANGEMENT

As is

TIME

30 minutes

DIRECTIONS

1. Players can sit at their usual places and share materials. Pass out a paper bag to each person and distribute scissors, glue, tape, and the decorative supplies.

2. Before players begin to decorate puppets, talk with everyone about an imaginary land from which all the puppets come. What kind of place is it? Do inhabitants live in the same manner as we do? What do they wear? What do they look like? What do they sound like? After some discussion about these puppet creatures, everyone can begin to make his or her own creature.

3. Encourage players to cut and paste paper and scraps rather than just draw with felt-tipped markers. Hair can be fringed paper, tongues can be cut fabric, and tails can be braided yarn. Fold a paper plate in half and attach it for an instant mouth, or use paper plates for ears and arms.

4. As more and more puppets from the imaginary land begin to invade the classroom they will probably begin to explore their new-found landscape. Students may interact with puppet gibberish or you may want to teach them a few games that we play here on our planet. Try sitting in a circle and letting the puppets play some games, such as No, No, No! (page 43) or A What? (page 51).

NEWSPAPER HEADGEAR

Some people wear hats to cover their heads, and some people wear hats to express themselves. Newspaper hats are not much protection against rain, sleet, or falling space junk, but they offer plenty of opportunity for some headstrong self-expression.

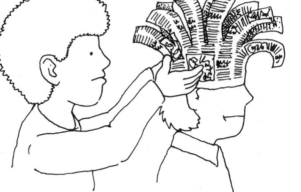

MATERIALS

Newspapers
Masking tape
Scissors
Staplers

ROOM ARRANGEMENT

Open space

TIME

25 minutes

DIRECTIONS

1. Push desks and chairs to the edges of the room and stack newspapers, tape, scissors, and staplers in the center. Players can work on the floor. Keep a wastepaper basket close by for cleanup.

2. Before everyone begins, talk with the group about hats. Make a list of the variety, such as chefs' hats, pirate hats, nurses' hats, Mickey Mouse hats, space helmets, feather headdresses, crowns, and so on.

3. Have each player take a sheet of newspaper and invent his or her own hat. Newspaper can be twisted into cones, cut into fringes, folded into caps, and made into any shape. Since newspaper is plentiful, allow players to use as much paper as they need.

4. When players are finished and the activity has gone to their heads, a hat parade with music is in order.

NEWSPAPER DOWELS

Old news is good news to newspaper recyclers.
Newspaper can become a great building
material that may make tomorrow's headlines.

MATERIALS

Newspapers
Masking tape

ROOM ARRANGEMENT

Open space

TIME

35 to 45 minutes

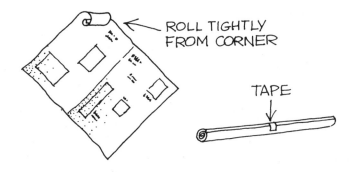

ROLL TIGHTLY FROM CORNER

TAPE

DIRECTIONS

1. Move furniture to the edges of the room and place a stack of newspapers in the middle. Demonstrate for players how to roll a single sheet of newspaper tightly into a dowel. Begin at one corner and roll diagonally, making it as hard and inflexible as possible. Tape the dowel to keep it from unrolling.

2. Join newspaper dowels together at ends with masking tape.

3. Players can build paper dowel structures on the floor. (Three dowels taped into a triangle are the strongest building unit, but allow players to experiment with different shapes.) Each player can construct his or her own structure, or everyone can work together on one gigantic construction that will fill the whole room. For added decoration fill in the framework with panels of colored paper and drawings.

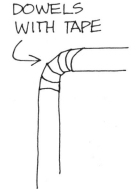

JOIN DOWELS WITH TAPE

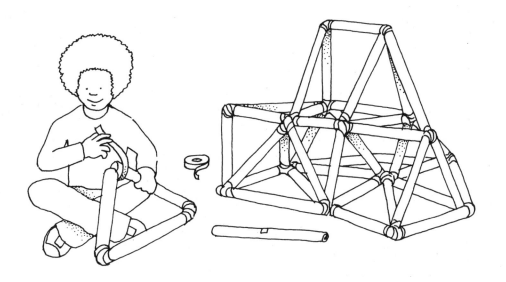

FAST FORESTS

This project will transform any room into a forest within minutes. It's an activity that can create a backdrop for an instant play or just a change of atmosphere.

MATERIALS

4 to 6 full-sized, double-spread sheets of newspaper for each player
Scissors

ROOM ARRANGEMENT

Open space

TIME

25 minutes

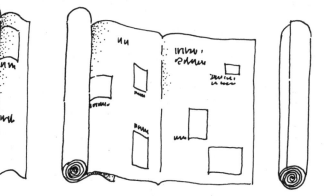

2.

DIRECTIONS

1. Give each player four to six sheets of newspaper. It is helpful if you demonstrate each step.
2. Roll a sheet up from a narrow end, leaving about two inches unrolled. Slip another sheet into the extended, unrolled piece and continue rolling. Do the same with a third and fourth sheet. The more newspaper sheets that are added, the larger the tree will be, but it becomes more difficult to cut. When the last piece of paper has been added, roll firmly.
3. Flatten one end of the roll and, using sharp scissors, cut halfway down the length of it.
4. Now flatten the same end so that the cuts are on the sides. Cut again in the center so that the end is now cut into quarters.
5. Hold the newspaper roll at the uncut end and shake, loosening the newspaper "leaves." Finding the center of the leaves, pull gently and watch the tree grow. To display trees in the room, tie a string across the room from wall to wall. Attach string to treetops and hang in a row.

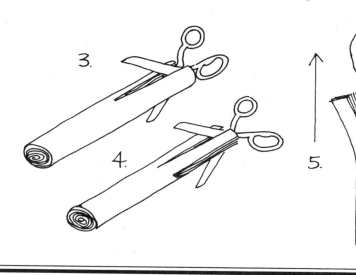

3.

4.

5.

GLIDERS

Although paper planes have been around for decades, this version is relatively new and has found much popularity among paper pilots.

MATERIALS

A plastic drinking straw for each player
2 paper clips for each player
A sheet of 4¼" x 11" construction paper for each player (8½" x 11" paper divided in half)
A pencil for each player
Rulers
Scissors

ROOM ARRANGEMENT

As is

TIME

20 minutes

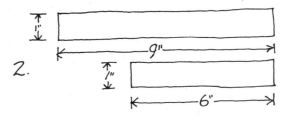

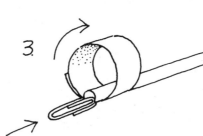

DIRECTIONS

1. Everyone may work at tables or desks. Give each player a drinking straw, a piece of paper, two paper clips, and a pencil. Have enough rulers and scissors on hand to share.

2. Each player cuts out two strips of paper, one strip 1" x 9" and the other 1" x 6". Players should write their names on one of the two strips to avoid any mix-ups later.

3. Slip one of the paper clips into one end of the straw. Make sure that the smaller wire loop is on the inside and the larger loop is on the outside. Slip the other clip on the other end in the same way. Roll each strip of paper into a loop and clip to either end of the straw, making sure that both paper loops are aligned.

4. When everyone is finished, it is time for a test flight. The suggested glider launch position is to hold the glider in the center with the small loop in front. Don't throw the glider, but gently push it forward so that it will sail. Adjustments can be made to the size of the larger loop to help give the smoothest flight possible.

WILD BLUE YONDER

The classic paper plane has been the same since the 1920s. Nearly every kid has made dozens, if not hundreds, of paper planes, but how many have thought of designing their own? In this activity players test their aeronautical engineering skills.

MATERIALS

As much paper as possible (at least 2 sheets of
    8½″ x 11″ paper for each player)
Scissors
Felt-tipped markers and crayons for additional
    decorating

ROOM ARRANGEMENT

Open space

TIME

30 to 40 minutes

DIRECTIONS

Part One: Test Pilot

  1. Give each player a sheet of paper. The object of this activity is to invent a new version of the classic paper plane. Players should try flying their unfolded paper to see how even a simple sheet of paper can float and stay aloft.

  2. Next, have players fold the paper in half to see what effects that has on its flight. Suggest that players try cutting their paper into the form of a plane, folding wings and edges for reinforcement.

  3. After players have explored the qualities of the paper and how it flies, give them another sheet of paper to make final paper planes. For extra help see Gliders, page 109, and Copters, page 112.

Part Two: Fly-Offs

  1. After pilots have tested and modified their creations, it's time for the Paper Plane Fly-Offs. Clear the room as much as possible. Move chairs and tables to make a launching area for planes. Those not flying planes should sit off to the side as spectators.

2. Judging paper planes can be fun if it is done in a playfully serious manner. Here are several categories:

- *Duration Aloft* Since few people carry a stopwatch and watching the second hand on a room clock is almost impossible, it is advisable to have all competitors line up and throw their entries at the same time. The last plane to land is the winner. Two out of three tries might be most fair for everyone.

- *Distance Flown* This is easier to judge. Players can fly planes one at a time, leaving them where they land. If there is a tie and both pilots hit the farthest wall, both will have to go again.

- *Aerobatics and Maneuverability* Hang a large hoop or box from the ceiling and see who can go through it or hit it. Create an obstacle course with a line of people. See how far planes can go under people's legs. Give pilots an opportunity to show off fancy flying tricks such as a loop-the-loop.

- *Most Inventive Design* Although some may not fly well they still may be great to look at. Have everyone vote for his or her favorite plane design. Winners can finish the fly-offs with their own mass launch.

COPTERS

Not all paper aircraft fly across the room from wall to wall. Some fly vertically. This aircraft may not be big on distance, but it is definitely lots of fun to watch.

MATERIALS

A sheet of 8½″ x 11″ paper for each player
A pencil for each player
Rulers
Scissors

ROOM ARRANGEMENT

As is

TIME

15 minutes

DIRECTIONS

1. Give each player a sheet of paper, pencil, ruler, and scissors. (Rulers and scissors can be shared if there are not enough for everyone.) You should demonstrate construction while giving instructions.

2. First, have each player measure and cut a 2″ x 11″ strip of paper. Halfway down the strip, cut two 1-inch slits into each side.

3. Next, cut a 4-inch slit from the top.

4. Fold the bottom stem to weight it.

5. Fold the top pieces in opposite directions for propellers.

6. After copters are completed, have everyone hold them upright and drop from a high place. Organize a mass launching by having players line up in two rows facing each other. On the count of three, have everyone drop the copters in a huge flurry of spinning paper.

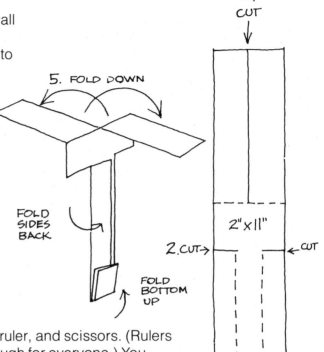

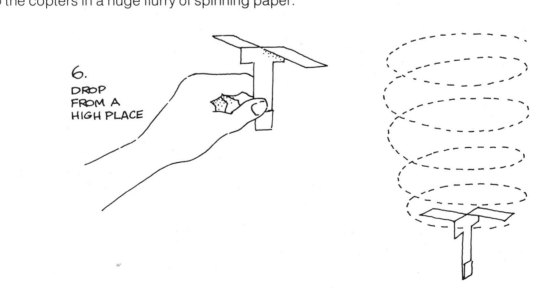

THINGS ARE PICKIN' UP

After a creative activity there are usually paper scraps, scissors, tape, and other materials all over the floor. Clean up usually isn't fun — unless it becomes a game. Here's a housekeeping game kids are sure to pick up on.

MATERIALS

Leftover scraps on the floor
2 brooms
2 trash bags
2 dust pans

ROOM ARRANGEMENT

A mess

TIME

5 minutes

DIRECTIONS

Method 1: Divide and Conquer

1. Divide the room into two sections and the group into two teams. Each team is given a trash bag, broom, dust pan, and any other necessary cleaning equipment.

2. The two teams line up in the center, face to face. When you say "Go!" both teams race to clean up their area and reassemble back in the center of the room.

3. The first team finished is the winner, but the title is not final until each team inspects the other team's section. If both teams turn up overlooked scraps on both sides, the game will have to be called a draw.

Method 2: Clean Sweep

1. The entire group lines up together in a cooperative team effort to beat the clock and be the fastest cleaners in the world!

2. Armed with brooms, trash bags, and dust pans, the group stands at attention as you eye the minute hand of the clock. When you say "Go!" the group scrambles to clean every square inch of the room — picking up papers, straightening furniture, and putting equipment back in place.

3. When the room is clean, record the amount of time the cleanup took — which will have to be beaten the next time the room is a mess.

Play on Words

I've got a wonderful sense of humor.

I'm a great dancer.

I'm helpful.

I'm friendly.

I bake the best brownies.

I love butterscotch sundaes.

I never complain.

I can play the piano with one finger.

TERRIBLE TELEGRAMS

Because each additional word costs extra money, telegrams usually use as few words as possible to get the message across. Often words such as *a, and,* and *the* are omitted. That's why telegrams can be a bit jumpy. In this game students try to telegraph messages as cheaply as possible.

MATERIALS

Chalkboard or large sheet of paper
Chalk or a felt-tipped marker
A sheet of standard-sized paper for each player
A pencil for each player

ROOM ARRANGEMENT

As is

TIME

20 to 30 minutes

DIRECTIONS

1. Give paper and a pencil to each player.
2. Each player says the first letter that comes to mind. As players recite random letters, write them in order of recitation on the chalkboard for everyone to see.
3. Each player must compose a telegram using each letter written on the board as the first letter of a new word. For example, the letters L T U V M K F E might become "Large tomatoes under van. Make ketchup for everyone" or "Like torn umbrellas very much. Keeping for elephants." Players should try to compose messages that make some kind of sense — however weird.
4. Telegrams should be folded and passed to other players. Allow players to read some of the terrible telegrams aloud.

POTS AND PANS

No, this game is not about kitchen utensils but about things that go together in pairs.

MATERIALS

A sheet of paper for each player
A pin for each player
A pencil

ROOM ARRANGEMENT

Open space

TIME

20 minutes

DIRECTIONS

1. This game takes a few moments of preparation. Make yourself a list of pairs of things. For example:

- ham and eggs
- pepper and salt
- shoes and socks
- stars and stripes
- bread and butter
- nickel and dime
- thunder and lightning
- Romeo and Juliet
- Lone Ranger and Tonto
- Tom Sawyer and Huck Finn
- Jack and Jill
- Roy Rogers and Trigger
- twist and shout
- birds and bees
- sticks and stones
- hook and ladder
- cops and robbers

2. On each piece of paper write the name of one member of each pair.

3. Gather players in a circle with their backs toward the center. Pin a sheet of paper to each back so that the person pinned does not know the word on his or her back.

4. After all players are pinned, each must try to find the person with the mate to his or her word. This is difficult because no player knows his or her own word and is not allowed to ask its identity directly. Players may ask each other any question at all ("Is it a person?" "Is it an animal?") except "What's my word?" Before finding partners, players must find out what their own words are.

5. The game ends when each player has successfully found his or her partner.

NAME·O·GRAMS

What's in a name? Lots of letters! Rearrange them and see if they still match their owners.

MATERIALS

A 3″ x 5″ file card for each player
A pencil for each player

ROOM ARRANGEMENT

As is

TIME

15 minutes

DIRECTIONS

1. Give each player a file card and a pencil.
2. Players print their names in reverse, for example, *Jane Jones* would become *Enaj Senoj.*
3. The leader collects the cards, shuffles them, and distributes them to the players.
4. One by one players read aloud the backward names they have received. The rest of the group must try to guess within ten seconds whose name it is.

VARIATION

1. Players print their names in scrambled order, mixing up letters to spell other words when possible. For example, *Thomas* might become *Hot Sam.*
2. Players fold cards and keep passing them until you say to stop.
3. Players unfold cards and begin to unscramble the name. When a player unscrambles a name, he or she searches for the player whose name it is. These players join hands. As more and more players' names are unscrambled, pairs become lines, lines join together, and soon there is one large, unscrambled circle.

MEANWHILE, BACK AT THE RANGH

In many movies, two or three stories happen at the same time. Scenes are intercut to show the various stories developing. While Groucho is off turning a swanky dinner party into a food fight, his brother Harpo is calmly playing his harp in the swimming pool.

MATERIALS

A sheet of standard-sized paper for each player
A pencil for each player

ROOM ARRANGEMENT

As is

TIME

15 minutes

DIRECTIONS

1. The entire group is seated at desks or tables. Each player is given a sheet of paper which is divided into three columns. The group agrees on three different subjects. For example, fruit, foreign countries, and animals might be chosen.

2. When you call out a column number, each player starts to write about the subject in that column. When you call another number, players stop in mid-sentence and begin to write about the subject in that column. Call out numbers randomly and rapidly: "One!" "Three!" "Two!" "Three!" "One!"

3. When sheets are nearly filled, call out "The end!" At this point players must try to connect all three stories and create some sort of finish. For example, "And so the baby grapefruit left home to see the world only to fall in love with the lonely walrus. They were married under the Eiffel Tower and lived happily ever after in Paris." Players who feel they have a funny or interesting story may want to read it to the group.

ONE AND ONLY

Each of us is unique, but in what ways do we show it? Here's a chance for players to reveal what sets them apart from everyone else.

MATERIALS

A 3″ x 5″ file card for each player
A pencil for each player

ROOM ARRANGEMENT

Open space

TIME

20 minutes

DIRECTIONS

1. Give players file cards and pencils and ask them to write descriptions of themselves. The descriptions must point out their unique qualities, experiences, or accomplishments — the things that make them unlike any other person in the group. It's better to describe personality than physical appearance. Players should not sign their names.

2. Collect file cards and shuffle them. Players form a circle and sit on the floor. File cards are passed out. If a player receives his or her own card, players close their eyes and switch cards.

3. One by one, players read the cards they are holding. After each reading, the group tries to guess who wrote it. The goal is to try to guess as quickly as possible the identity of the unique person.

I've got a wonderful sense of humor.

I'm a great dancer.

I'm helpful.

I'm friendly.

I bake the best brownies.

I never complain.

I love butterscotch sundaes.

I can play the piano with one finger.

A LONG STORY

This experiment in cooperative storytelling may not only become the world's longest story, but also the tallest one!

MATERIALS

A roll of business machine paper (used with adding machines, cash registers, and so on)
A pencil for each player

ROOM ARRANGEMENT

Open space

TIME

15 to 25 minutes

DIRECTIONS

1. Arrange players in a single line, side by side, and have them sit on the floor. Give each player a pencil. Roll out a ribbon of white business machine paper across the floor in front of the players.

2. Each player is limited to adding three words in each turn to the story line. One by one, players add their words, connecting them to the words of the last player. Players can read the last few words before making an addition, but they should not worry about making perfect sense.

3. After a player adds three words, he or she can go to the end of the line for another turn. It's up to you how long the story gets to be and how many turns the group should have.

4. The last player to add something can add the last few words to finish the sentence. Four or five readers should take turns and read the story aloud to the group.

HIDDEN TREASURES

To this day, the lure of hidden treasure prompts people to explore the depths of the oceans and the jungles of uncharted lands. This activity is designed to turn an everyday room into a treasure chest.

MATERIALS

2 sheets of any available paper for each player
A pencil for each player

ROOM ARRANGEMENT

As is

TIME

40 minutes

DIRECTIONS

1. Pass two sheets of paper and a pencil to each player.
2. Tell each person to draw a treasure secretly without letting anyone else see. Suggest it be something very special, maybe something not even invented yet — like a round-trip ticket to Mars. Or it could be something that everyone dreams about — a castle in the mountains, a supersonic race car, or a million dollars tax free!

3. When everyone is finished, have players fold their treasures into tiny packets. Next, each player should put a special mark on his or her treasure — an initial or symbol — which will identify it when it's found.

4. Players must hide their treasures in the classroom — under a book, behind a table, among the leaves of a plant, under a wastepaper basket — someplace out of sight but not impossible to find.

5. After treasures are hidden, players gather back at their desks. Have them use the other sheets of paper to draw maps and clues to help other players locate their hidden treasures. Suggest that clues be kept clear and simple. For example, "Start at the door by the sink. Take three steps toward the chalkboard. Turn right and walk five steps. Look under the table." Make sure that everyone includes the secret symbol on the map so that explorers will be able to identify the proper treasure.

6. Next, have players fold maps and tear them in half. Collect both halves and put them into some type of container. Have each player select two parts. Before the search can begin, players must match the two halves of one map.

7. As treasures are found, make certain that symbols match. When a player finds a treasure that does not match, the treasure must be replaced and the search continued. The game ends when every treasure is found.

SENTENCE RELAY

Even though this game is just for fun, it easily could be used as part of a language lesson.

MATERIALS

Chalkboard or three large sheets of butcher paper
3 felt-tipped markers or crayons

ROOM ARRANGEMENT

Open space

TIME

20 minutes

DIRECTIONS

1. Divide players into three teams and have them sit on the floor.
2. Draw vertical lines on the chalkboard to divide it into three sections. If no chalkboard is available, tack three large sheets of butcher paper to the wall.
3. Each team is seated about six feet from its part of the chalkboard or paper. Teams arrange themselves in the order in which each player is to run.
4. At your command the first member of each team races toward the chalkboard or paper, picks up the chalk or marker, and writes the first word of a sentence. The player then runs back to the team and hands the chalk or marker to the next runner. This new player then writes the next word to the sentence, and so on.
5. The first team whose last player completes a full sentence with all words spelled correctly is the winner. If all team members have participated but the sentence is incomplete, the rotation begins again with the first player until the sentence is finished. Runners may correct mistakes of previous teammates while they are at the chalkboard.

MAKE A LIST

During the year it is helpful to have ongoing activities — ones that can be picked up and put down on a moment's notice during a break or an in-between time when a game cannot be played. This activity becomes more and more of a challenge as it continues, and yet can be available at all times.

MATERIALS

A roll of paper (brown wrapping paper or any large roll of paper that can be written on)
A felt-tipped marker, a crayon, or any writing implement
Tape or tacks

ROOM ARRANGEMENT

As is

TIME

Ongoing

DIRECTIONS

1. Choose a free wall and tape or tack up a large piece of paper. Find an area where it can stay up all the time so players can add to it in free moments.

2. Select a category — something that might be fun and will allow for inventive interpretations. Some examples:

- *List things that are associated with the number 3.*
  Some of the things on the list might be: little pigs, blind mice, coins in a fountain, wise men, men in a tub, bears, primary colors (red, yellow, blue), triangle, tricycle, peas in a pod, three-ring circus, Columbus's boats, digits in an area code, three strikes and you're out.

- *Make a list of wet things.*
  Some of the things on this list might be: frogs, whales, gold fish, snow, orange juice, milk, tears, dog's nose, bottom of a boat, car wash, sink, egg yolk, peaches, tongues, eyeballs, ink, mud, worms, pickles, perspiration, runny nose.

- *Make a list of little-known statistics or trivial wonders.*
  Some people might have to go do some digging in almanacs, magazines, newspapers, or a book of world records to find things such as:
  a porcupine is equipped with about 18,000 quills, the standard 7-inch pencil will draw a line 35 miles long, Americans use a half billion hairpins a year, Americans swallow 3 billion quarts of ice cream and 16 billion aspirin tablets every year.

Thrills and Skills

GROUP JUGGLE

It's not new to see kids throwing crushed paper balls. It is new to encourage it as a game.

MATERIALS

6 or 7 crushed paper balls

ROOM ARRANGEMENT

Open space

TIME

15 minutes

DIRECTIONS

1. Everyone stands in a circle about one arm's length apart.
2. The first player throws a crushed paper ball to someone on the other side of the circle, who throws it to a third person, and so forth. This continues until the ball makes its way to everyone once and returns to the original person. Each player should receive the ball only once. Players are to remember to whom they throw the ball. When a pattern is set it is never broken throughout the game.
3. The leader throws the first ball. As the rhythm of the pattern becomes smoother and throwers and receivers get used to it, another ball is added, then a third, then a fourth. Players should be able, depending on the size of the group, to keep six or seven balls moving at once.
4. To help keep the rhythm of the group moving in a steady flow, try having everyone sing a song, such as "Row, Row, Row Your Boat," or repeat a silly chant — "Pass the ball, not the wall!" — that follows the beats of catching and throwing.

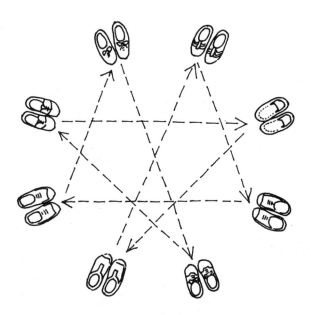

HAVABALL

This indoor game demands fast reflexes and agility. It's also safe and easy to play.

MATERIALS

2 rubber balls (beach balls, soft sponge balls, or balloons)

ROOM ARRANGEMENT

Open space

TIME

15 minutes

DIRECTIONS

1. Divide players into two equal teams. Teams stand in two facing lines about three feet apart.

2. Alternate members of each team change places with the player opposite so that each player faces a member of the opposing team and has a member of the opposing team on either side.

3. Give a ball to each team at one end of the two lines. Each person says "Havaball" and throws or passes the ball to the team member diagonally opposite.

4. When each ball reaches the end of the line, it is passed back in the opposite direction. Passing the ball from one end of the line to the other continues as many times as agreed upon before the game. Any fumbling or dropping will slow down the passing and put the other team in the lead.

5. The first team to complete passing the ball the agreed number of rounds is the winner.

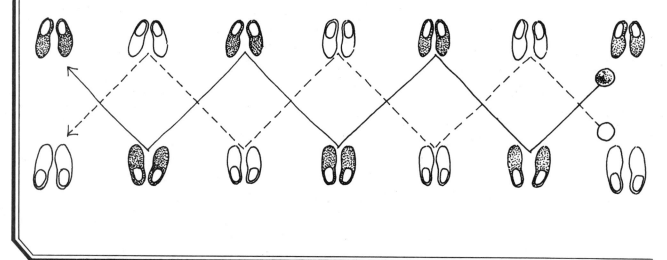

PERPETUAL MOTION

By playing this game, your group can go for a spin without leaving the room.

MATERIALS
A Frisbee or a metal plate

ROOM ARRANGEMENT
Open space

TIME
15 minutes

DIRECTIONS

1. Players sit in a circle on the floor and count off so that each person has a number. Place a Frisbee or a metal plate on the floor in the center of the circle.

2. The first player gets up, turns the disc on edge and spins it as you would a coin. As the player sits down he or she calls out the number of another player. The player whose number is called jumps up, gets the disc before it stops, gives it another spin, and calls out another player's number before sitting down.

3. Players continue calling each other's numbers and keeping the disc spinning. If the disc completely stops spinning, a player starts it again. The object of the game is to cooperate in keeping the disc spinning, not to trick other players.

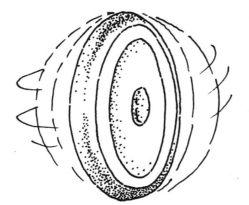

SLIPPED DISC

Without a doubt this game is much more fun than its name suggests.

MATERIALS

A Frisbee, a plastic plate, or a metal cover

ROOM ARRANGEMENT

Open space

TIME

15 minutes

DIRECTIONS

1. Everyone forms a circle on hands and knees with heads facing inward.

2. An object, such as a Frisbee, plastic plate, or metal cover, is placed in the middle of one person's back. The object of the game is to pass the object around the circle, from back to back, without using hands.

3. If the object falls, it is picked up by hand and placed on the back of the last person who had it. The game continues until the disc is passed successfully around the entire circle.

SOUNDS IN THE NIGHT

Late at night, animal sounds drift into the darkened house — dogs howling, crickets chirping, cats crying. In this game, the animals are indoors and play a noisy game of ball.

MATERIALS

A beach ball or a basketball

ROOM ARRANGEMENT

Open space

TIME

15 minutes

DIRECTIONS

1. Everyone sits in a circle with eyes closed. The room is darkened. Each player selects an animal sound to mimic as his or her own personal signal. If group members run out of animals from which to choose, divide players into separate game groups.

2. The first player has the ball and makes his or her animal sound and then the sound of the animal to whom he or she wants to roll the ball. The animal who is "called" replies so that the first player knows where to direct the ball. The first player then rolls the ball to that animal.

3. If the intended player receives the ball, he or she responds loudly. All the other animals rejoice in unison by making their sounds also. However, if the intended player misses, the ball goes back to the first player who tries another animal.

HOT STUFF

This is a variation of the game Hot Potato. In the original game, the person who is caught holding the potato is out. In this game nobody is eliminated, just rearranged.

MATERIALS

A ball or a balloon

ROOM ARRANGEMENT

Open space

TIME

15 minutes

DIRECTIONS

1. Move furniture and obstacles aside. Gather everyone in a circle.
2. One person is chosen as the Caller. Before each round, the Caller stands outside the circle and secretly picks a number from 1 to 50. As the players stand in the circle, passing the ball from player to player, the Caller counts aloud to the preselected number, then yells "Hot stuff!"
3. Meanwhile, the players in the circle must keep the ball moving from player to player. When the Caller yells "hot stuff," the person with the ball (or if the ball is between players, the person just about to catch the ball) leaves the circle and joins the Caller.
4. As more and more players leave the circle, the Caller group becomes larger and larger, and the counting becomes louder and louder. The original Caller tells the new Callers the number to which the group will count.
5. As the game dwindles to two players passing the ball back and forth, the last person left without the ball when the callers yell "hot stuff" will be the winner.

LASER GUN

In a darkened room a flashlight can become a nonlethal light saber. Players caught in the beam before they reach home base are frozen in place.

MATERIALS

A flashlight

ROOM ARRANGEMENT

Open space

TIME

15 minutes

DIRECTIONS

1. The room becomes the far reaches of outer space. Darken it as much as possible by pulling window shades, covering doors, and turning off lights. One person is chosen to be the Space Patrol and stands guard over the five-foot-square space station in the center of the room with a trusty laser gun (flashlight).

2. The person who is acting as the Space Patrol closes his or her eyes and counts slowly to fifty as everyone hides. The object of the game is to try to get to the space station in the center of the room without getting tagged with the beam from the laser gun.

3. If space invaders dare to make a run for the space station and get caught by the laser gun light beam, they are instantly frozen in space forever — or at least until the end of the game. The first person to get to the space station without getting caught is the next Space Patrol.

SPOT CHECK

This game is reminiscent of Pin the Tail on the Donkey without the tail and the donkey.

MATERIALS

A key, a button, a coin, or any other small object
A small pad of paper
Masking tape
A pencil for each player

ROOM ARRANGEMENT

Open space

TIME

15 minutes

DIRECTIONS

1. Clear the center of the room and place a small object — a key, a button, a coin, or whatever — on the floor in the center.
2. Each player writes his or her name on a small slip of paper and connects a piece of masking tape to it. At one end of the room, a starting line is marked with a line of tape.
3. One by one, players are blindfolded, turned around a few times, and told to walk to the spot where they think the object is located without actually touching the object.
4. When the player reaches the spot, he or she is allowed one chance to tape the slip of paper next to it. The game continues until each player has had a turn. The player whose paper is closest to the spot is the winner.

WASTEPAPER BASKETBALL

When the ancient Mayan game using a ball and a hoop was formalized in 1891 by Dr. James Naismith and called *basketball*, little did anyone realize that the game would be further amended by young inventors using paper balls and wastepaper baskets.

MATERIALS

2 wastepaper baskets or cardboard boxes
Crushed paper balls

ROOM ARRANGEMENT

As is

TIME

25 minutes

DIRECTIONS

1. In this game, players must remain in their seats. Divide the group into two teams by counting off. Two wastepaper baskets or cardboard boxes are placed at opposite corners of the room, one for each team.

2. Players can shoot from anywhere or can pass the paper ball to each other, trying to get it to the teammate closest to the basket. Opposing team members can try to intercept shots, just as long as there is no physical contact. You can award free shots when fouls occur.

3. Referees should be stationed at each end of the room to retrieve stray paper balls and throw them back to players.

4. If the defending team intercepts a pass or retrieves the ball after a shot misses the basket, it keeps possession of the ball. After a team makes a basket, the ball goes to the other team.

5. Use a new paper ball after each basket. After an agreed-upon number of plays or amount of time, the team with the most paper balls in its basket is the winner.

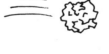

VARIATION

You may want to try a balloon instead of a paper ball.

BALLOON SOCCER

Traditional outdoor games that are too vigorous for indoor play can be adapted simply by changing equipment and altering the rules a bit. After you've played this version of soccer, ask players to think of ways other games might be changed in order to be played safely indoors.

MATERIALS

12 balloons (or more if you like)
2 pins

ROOM ARRANGEMENT

As is

TIME

25 minutes

DIRECTIONS

1. All players sit in rows evenly spaced throughout the room. Two goalies sit at opposite corners of the room. Both goalies have pushpins, safety pins, or other instruments that will break balloons. The rest of the group is divided into two teams by counting off.
2. To begin, the leader drops an inflated balloon in the center of the room. Each team tries to hit the balloon to its goalie, who remains in a corner.
3. The goalie who gets the balloon and pops it scores a point for the team. This game is also fun without keeping score. There is a great deal of status in being a balloon-popping goalie. Make sure that many players have a chance to do it.

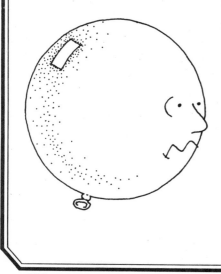

BALLOONING

A balloon's not much really — a bit of air wrapped in a bright package. It's not so much a toy as a possibility, an invitation to the imagination. Here are some breath-taking balloonisms.

MATERIALS

At least one balloon for each player
Masking tape

ROOM ARRANGEMENT

Open space

TIME

30 minutes

DIRECTIONS

1. Have players stand in a circle and give each player a balloon.
2. Instruct players to blow up their balloons but not to tie them. Start the ballooning event with a balloon band playing "The Raspberry Serenade." (Players won't need any help in "playing" their balloons.) See if any of the balloonists can play recognizable melodies.
3. After this rousing overture, tape an X on the floor in the center of the circle. Players inflate balloons again but do not tie them. One by one, players release balloons, seeing how close each can come to the X.
4. Players retrieve balloons and tape a boundary line on either end of the room. For this part of the activity, inflate five balloons and tie them. Divide the group into five teams. All teams line up single file behind one of the boundaries. This is a balloon relay game. The first member of each team is given a balloon. At the leader's signal, they must bat their balloons across the room and back again to the next team member in line. If a balloon touches the floor, the player must go back and start from the beginning. The first team to finish is the winner.
5. Next, have players inflate and tie all the balloons. The leader gathers all the balloons in one corner and, one by one, tosses them to the group. The group must not let any balloon touch the floor. For an added challenge, suggest that players not use their hands.
6. To end with a big blast, allow players to sit on their balloons and pop them all at once.

THE GHOST GAME

How many players could recognize the spirit of a friend who returned as a ghost? Here's a chance to find out.

MATERIALS

An old bed sheet or large piece of fabric

ROOM ARRANGEMENT

Open space

TIME

15 minutes

DIRECTIONS

  1. Divide the group into two teams.
  2. One team is chosen to leave the room and send back one of its members draped in a sheet.
  3. The "ghost" should try to augment the disguise by crouching to look smaller or stretching to look taller or wider. Make sure that nothing is visible (shoes or pants) to give the ghost's identity away.
  4. The guessing team cannot touch the ghost. After a short consultation, the team is allowed one chance to guess the ghost's identity.
  5. If the guess is wrong, another ghost from the same team comes in. If the guess is correct, the two teams change sides.

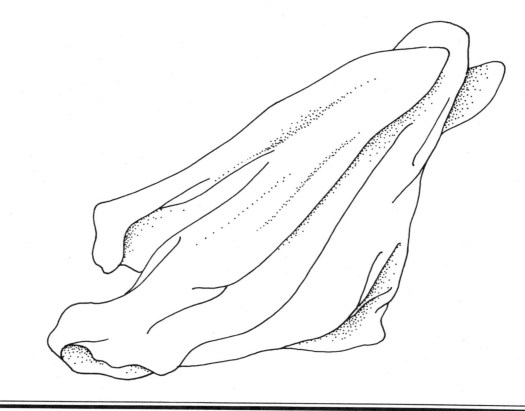

ONE-ACT PLAYS

Every now and then you may need a quick activity that takes very little explanation and can be performed in minutes. Each of these three activities can be done in less than five minutes.

MATERIALS
A nickel
A potato chip, a piece of popcorn, or a piece of soft candy
2 peanuts

ROOM ARRANGEMENT
Open space

TIME
Less than 5 minutes each

DIRECTIONS
Nickel Nose
Borrow a nickel and ask a volunteer to lie down on the floor. Place the nickel on the person's nose and tell him or her to wiggle the nickel off by wrinkling nose and face. No head movements are allowed for this nearly impossible act.

Chip Away
Place a potato chip, piece of popcorn, or small piece of candy on a player's shoulder. The player must try to remove the morsel with his or her tongue.

Nosed Out
Select two players to have a race by rolling peanuts across the floor with their noses. Put lines of tape on the floor for the start and finish. In this game, the winner always wins by a nose.

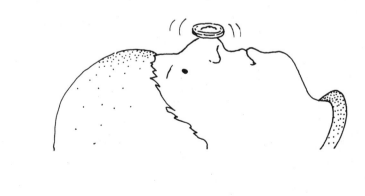

WORLD CHAMPION PAPER-STACKING CONTEST

Skyscrapers are exciting symbols of human ability and imagination. This skyscraping activity requires plenty of both.

MATERIALS

As much scrap paper as possible

ROOM ARRANGEMENT

Open space

TIME

20 to 30 minutes

DIRECTIONS

1. Clear a large, open space in the room. Divide the group into two teams or into several small ones.

2. Each team gets an equal pile of paper with which to build a tower. No other materials — no staplers, tape, or glue — can be used to construct the tower. Papers should be folded to reinforce construction. The tighter the paper is folded, the stronger it gets — but it also gets smaller. Loosely folded paper might provide large building elements, but the construction will be more fragile.

3. The team that builds the highest tower wins an award. Award citations also for the cleverest construction techniques and the most architecturally beautiful.

VARIATION

Have the entire group work together to build the world's largest paper building.

PIPE LINE

People have smoked pipes, have had pipe dreams, and even followed pied pipers. Now here's a pipe game to play.

MATERIALS

A sheet of 9" x 12" construction paper for each player
2 paper clips for each player
2 small crushed paper balls or any 2 small round objects

ROOM ARRANGEMENT

Open space

TIME

10 minutes

ROLL PAPER INTO A CYLINDER

FASTEN ENDS WITH PAPER CLIPS

DIRECTIONS

1. Give each person a piece of construction paper and two paper clips. Have players roll their papers into 12-inch cylinders with a 1-inch overlap. Fasten ends with paper clips.

2. Separate the group into two teams and have them stand in two parallel lines. Tell teams to hold their paper cylinders end to end to create a long pipe.

3. Crush two pieces of paper into balls small enough to fit through the cylinders. Say "Go!" and drop the paper balls into the ends of the first two cylinders. Team members must jiggle the paper balls from one cylinder to the next. If a paper ball drops on the floor, the last person must pick it up and try again. Passes can only be made from cylinder to cylinder.

4. When the paper ball gets to the last person's cylinder, teams must reverse the passing. The first team to get the paper ball back to the beginning is the winner.

KANGAROO RELAY

Players will jump for joy when you ask them to hop to it in this game.

MATERIALS

A basketball, a beach ball, or a balloon

ROOM ARRANGEMENT

Open space

TIME

10 minutes

DIRECTIONS

1. Divide the group into two teams and have players line up, one behind the other. Place a chair about ten feet in front of each team.

2. The first players place a ball between their knees, hop around the chair, and return to tag the next players in line. Players may touch the ball with their hands to pass it to the next player or to pick it up when dropped, but they cannot move while touching the ball with their hands.

3. The first team to send every member around the chair and back is the winner.

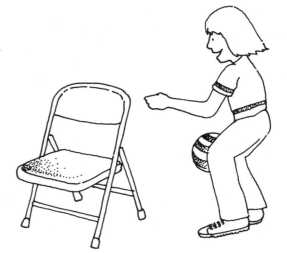

NEWSPAPER RELAY

This is not a game in which to be footloose and fancy-free, but rather to be as surefooted as possible.

MATERIALS

Newspapers

ROOM ARRANGEMENT

Open space

TIME

20 minutes

DIRECTIONS

1. Divide the group into two teams.
2. Fold several sheets of newspaper into quarters to create a solid pad on which to step. Each team will need two pads.
3. Give the first person on each team two folded newspaper pads.
4. Define the starting line behind which teams must stand, and select a goal across the room.
5. When the leader signals, the first player on each team must put down a newspaper pad and step on it, then put down the other newspaper pad and step on that one, then pick up the first and put it farther ahead to step on, and so on, until the player reaches the goal. The process is repeated while returning.
6. On returning, the first player touches the next player in line. The next player continues in the same fashion.
7. The first team to finish wins the relay.

ROPE RELAY

This is the kind of game in which being a slippery character pays off!

MATERIALS

Two 3-foot pieces of rope or heavy yarn

ROOM ARRANGEMENT

Open space

TIME

15 minutes

DIRECTIONS

  1. Tie ropes into loops big enough to fit over the biggest player in the group.

  2. Divide the group into two lines. Each line is a team. To add some team spirit, have each line pick a name, such as the Super Loopers or the Silver Slippers.

  3. Give the first person on each team a rope loop. The object of the game is to have each person slip through the loop and pass it along for each of the following players to slip through.

  4. A referee should make sure everyone goes through. The first team that gets every player through the loop is the winner.

SPINNING A YARN

Here's a game that will transform a room of players into a closely knit group.

MATERIALS

A ball of thick yarn

ROOM ARRANGEMENT

Open space

TIME

5 to 10 minutes

DIRECTIONS

1. Players stand together randomly in a group.
2. One player takes a ball of thick yarn and wraps the end around his or her waist, and then passes the ball to another person.
3. The next player wraps it around his or her waist, and continues to pass the ball of yarn to another player, and so forth.
4. Once the entire group has been all bound up in the yarn, the whole group process is reversed, but this time players close their eyes. The last player unwraps himself or herself, rewinds the ball, and hands it to the next player, and so on, until the rewound ball reaches the first player again.

FORGE FIELD

An entire group is trapped inside the electric force field. Will they be able to work together in a spirit of cooperation and escape? Tune in to this game and find out!

MATERIALS

20 to 30 feet of clothesline rope

ROOM ARRANGEMENT

Open space

TIME

20 minutes

DIRECTIONS

  1. Divide the room in half by tying a rope from one side to the other, about three feet off the floor. Gather the entire group on one side of the rope.

  2. The rope represents an electric force field. Players who accidentally touch it are zapped with electricity, must fall to the floor, and must remain there for the rest of the game. The object of the game is to get everyone from one side of the fence to the other without getting zapped.

  3. This problem demands group cooperation. Players cannot jump but must work together to lift each other carefully over the force field. To help, only one object can be used — a chair or desk to stand on or a broom held by players on either side to assist the climb. Be careful that players do not throw each other over the force field and that the last person doesn't dive over it.

VARIATION

For older children it's fun to play Force Field in total silence as if it were a secret escape. Players will have to pantomime instructions to each other.

STRINGING ALONG

This game will strike a positive cord. Players will need sharp vision, nimble fingers, and a thread of hope.

MATERIALS

A ball of string

ROOM ARRANGEMENT

As is

TIME

15 minutes

DIRECTIONS

1. Cut 75 to 100 pieces of string of varying lengths — from 2 inches to several feet. Hide each piece of string someplace in the room before players arrive.

2. Have players stand in the middle of the room. Divide the group into two teams and explain that you've hidden pieces of string, pointing out the more obvious ones.

3. The object of the game is for each team to find and tie together as many strings as possible. Since the strings are not the same length, the winning team will not necessarily be the one with the largest number of strings, but the one with the longest line.

4. When it seems that most strings have been found and tied, have teams stretch their lines of string next to each other to compare. The team with the longest string is the winner.

MULTIPLE HOPSCOTCH

Those who have always avoided stepping on a crack so as not to break Mother's back will probably like Multiple Hopscotch. These three hopscotch grids are easy to make and the games presented can be changed to fit specific groups. Children will play on them without any outside organization. A plus: the grids look very nice when they are not being used.

MATERIALS

3 to 6 rolls of masking tape for each board
Scissors
A tape measure or yardstick
Chalk or a pencil

ROOM ARRANGEMENT

Open space

TIME

60 minutes to construct a game board
10 minutes for group activities

DIRECTIONS

X Grid

1. Tape the grid on the floor.
2. Divide the group into two teams. Divide team members into pairs. An extra player can be a caller.
3. The first two pairs stand arm in arm on the double squares at opposite ends of the board. Each player stands on one foot. The object of the game is to hop to the middle, one square at a time, then turn right and hop down the other arm of the game board.
4. When you say "Go," the two pairs hop toward the center. The first pair to reach the center gets to use the four middle squares first in order to turn while the other team waits.
5. After both pairs pass the center and are hopping down opposite arms, the next pairs of hoppers can go. The first team to get all team members to the end is the winner.

X GRID

Woven Grid

1. Tape the grid on the floor.

2. Divide the group into four teams. Each team picks a side of the game board. The object of the game is to hop on one foot from one side of the game board to the other and then reassemble. Large teams may have to take two separate turns.

3. When you say "Go," everyone starts to hop through the grid, trying not to bump into other players. To make hopping routes more of a challenge certain squares can be marked "out of bounds" with colored paper or tape.

4. The first team to reassemble on the opposite side is the winner.

Stepped Grid

1. Tape the grid on the floor. The squares on two adjacent sides should add up to enough spaces for the entire group.

2. Divide the group into two teams, one team standing on one side of the grid and the other team on the opposite side.

3. When you say "Go," both teams hop across the grid to the opposite side, each player on one foot, without bumping into other players.

4. Players who hop into a square with another player already in it will have to go back and start over. The first team to reassemble on the opposite end is the winner.

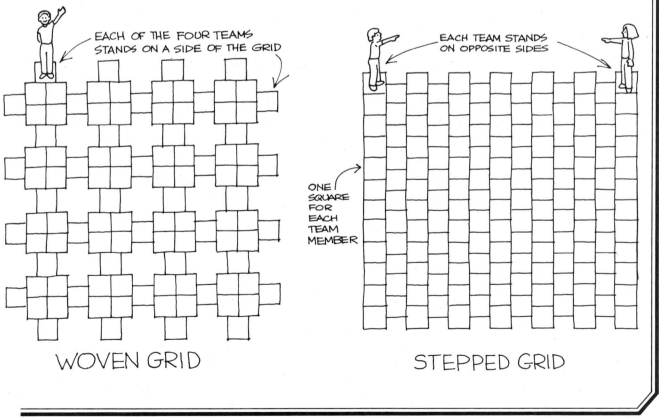

EACH OF THE FOUR TEAMS STANDS ON A SIDE OF THE GRID

EACH TEAM STANDS ON OPPOSITE SIDES

ONE SQUARE FOR EACH TEAM MEMBER

WOVEN GRID

STEPPED GRID

PART THREE
Plan Ahead

Using an assortment of materials, such as cardboard boxes, bolts of fabric, rolls of foil, and other specially collected supplies, players have the chance to explore all sorts of possibilities. Play becomes a self-motivated process of creative discovery, physical investigation, and intellectual challenge rather than a highly structured game.

Food, Foil, Fabric, and Faces

BREAD PAINTINGS

Here's an activity that is not only fun to do but good to eat. Bread paintings can transform any everyday sandwich into a work of art using materials found in almost any kitchen.

MATERIALS

2 slices of white bread for each player
Assorted food colorings
2 quarts of milk
A paper cup for each player
A new paint brush for each player *or* a supply of cotton-tipped swabs
Toaster

ROOM ARRANGEMENT

Individual work areas for each group of five or six players

TIME

30 to 40 minutes

DIRECTIONS

1. Have the players form groups of five or six. Supply each group with five or six paper cups filled with small amounts of milk. Add a little food coloring to each cup of milk. Give each player two slices of bread.

2. Players should use new brushes or cotton-tipped swabs to apply the milk-paint. To keep colors bright, tell players to keep brushes separate and not mix colors.

3. This is a good project to experiment with different painting styles. Try scribbling a design with one color, then fill in the spaces with other colors and patterns. Brush stripes in one direction with one color, then brush stripes of another color at right angles to create a plaid pattern. Draw pictures of stars and rainbows or just cover the bread with multicolored dots. Be careful not to get bread too soaked with milk.

4. Dry the bread paintings in a toaster set for light toast. When everyone has finished making edible art, other transformations will happen with each bite.

SNACK-FOOD SCULPTURE

The history of snack food as we know it probably began with the first television commercial when millions of people ran to the kitchen in search of fast treats — and back in time for the rest of their favorite show. While doing this activity, players build more than just an appetite.

MATERIALS

4 or 5 different kinds of snack food (bread sticks, pretzels, rippled potato chips, corn chips, cheese curls, popcorn, crackers, and so forth)
Three 8-ounce packages of cream cheese
8 ounces of sour cream
1 package of dried onion soup mix
Mixing bowl
Mixing spoon
A plastic knife for each player
A paper plate for each player

ROOM ARRANGEMENT

As is

TIME

30 to 40 minutes

DIRECTIONS

1. Before making snack-food sculptures, prepare the "paste" to stick pieces together. Mix three 8-ounce packages of softened cream cheese with 8 ounces of sour cream. Blend in a package of dried onion soup mix.

2. Divide the players into groups of five or six. Give each group an assortment of snack foods — bread sticks, pretzels, crackers, and so forth — and some paste. Each player should have a paper plate and a plastic knife.

3. Before pasting snack food together with the onion soup mixture, lay out pieces on the paper plates as a framework for construction. Snack foods such as bread sticks, pretzels, crackers, and rippled potato chips are structurally sound and are good for foundations. To build tall structures, use bread sticks as a skeleton and add lighter foods, such as cheese curls, on top.

4. If the finished basic structure seems strong enough, decorate the surface with popcorn, crackers, and taco chips. Try repeating a row of cheese puffs across the top or sticking pretzel bits off the side.

5. When snack-food sculptures are finished, they should be displayed. Organize a snack-food parade with the sculptures as floats. At parade's end, snack-food sculptures can be eaten — artfully nibbled into nothingness.

FOILING AROUND

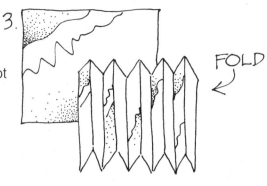

FOLD

Aluminum foil is very practical — and it's also a lot of fun. In this activity players won't mind being foilish.

MATERIALS

Roll of heavy-duty aluminum foil
Scissors
Cellophane tape
Medium-weight string

ROOM ARRANGEMENT

As is

PINCH →

TIME

30 minutes

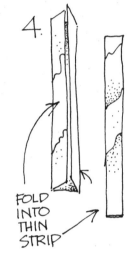

4.

FOLD INTO THIN STRIP

DIRECTIONS

1. Tie several pieces of medium-weight string across the room to hang decorations as they are completed.

2. Give each player a 3-foot sheet of foil. Players can share scissors and cellophane tape.

3. Aluminum foil fans are made by cutting a rectangle of foil approximately 9″ x 12″, folding it into an accordian, and pinching the center together.

4. Curls are made by first folding a long sheet of foil into a thin strip, then twisting the strip around a broom handle or dowel. Remove the molded curl.

CURL →

5. Foil chains are fun to construct with several players. Cut some foil into 8-inch squares. Roll up a square into a long thin stick, holding one end open with a finger. Form the foil stick into a circle, slipping the slender end into the open end and then crushing them together. Continue to connect foil circles into a long chain that can loop across the ceiling.

6. A circular fringe is a bit more complicated. Fold a 12″ x 20″ sheet of foil in half the long way. Place a sheet of paper between the folded sheet (for cutting ease) and cut in from the folded side. Only cut to about 1 inch from the outer edges. Remove the sheet of paper and roll the foil around a dowel to remove the crease. Tape the ends together to form a circle.

7. Encourage players to crush foil scraps into any and all sorts of shapes. For added effects, turn a rotating, colored spot light on the foil decorations and turn off overhead lights.

ROLL 5.

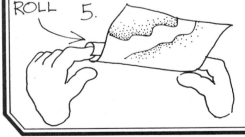

CRUSH

CIRCLE AND SQUEEZE ENDS TOGETHER

FOILED AGAIN!

Students will really be able to get into this activity as they mold full-scale portraits of each other with aluminum foil.

MATERIALS

Roll of heavy-duty aluminum foil
Scissors
Cellophane tape

ROOM ARRANGEMENT

Open space

TIME

30 minutes

DIRECTIONS

1. Before players begin, cut two sheets of foil about five feet long for each player.

2. Separate the group into pairs. Each player should tape the two sheets of foil together in order to have a sheet large enough to cover a single person.

3. One player of each pair lies on the floor. The other player places the sheet over his or her supine partner, slowly molding the foil around arms, legs, torso, and head. Extra care should be given when molding around the head to avoid hurting the person under the foil.

4. Foil is lifted off very carefully. Excess foil can be trimmed away with scissors. Scraps should be saved for future foil sculptures.

5. Foil figures can be hung with string from the ceiling or tacked directly to the wall. Try molding several players at once into a three-headed, six-legged, six-armed monster. Foil figures add a glamorous gallery of glittering ghosts to gloomy rooms.

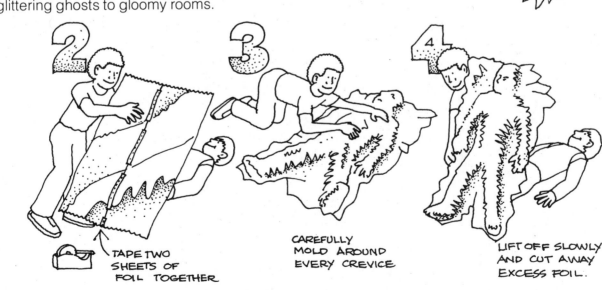

TAPE TWO SHEETS OF FOIL TOGETHER

CAREFULLY MOLD AROUND EVERY CREVICE

LIFT OFF SLOWLY AND CUT AWAY EXCESS FOIL.

GROUP LOOP

Some activities tie people together more than other activities. This one bands them and springs them into action.

MATERIALS
Bolt of fabric, 10 to 15 yards long

ROOM ARRANGEMENT
Open space

TIME
15 minutes

DIRECTIONS
1. Securely tie the ends of the long bolt of fabric together so that it forms a large loop.
2. Have players step inside the loop and face the center, spacing themselves equally and pulling the loop up behind them. Players should step back and lean on the inside of the fabric, stretching it taut enough to support everyone.
3. With the fabric stretched tightly, have players roll slowly against it in one direction, then reverse and roll the opposite way.
4. Divide the group into four sections. The two sections across from each other release the fabric and switch places. As the fabric is released the other two groups stretch the fabric to take up the slack. As the two teams reassemble and lean on the fabric again, it will stretch and the other two sections will be drawn toward the center. The two teams across from each other alternate with the other two teams that face each other, beginning slowly to set up a rhythm of switch and stretch.

WRAP-UPS

Children often like to decorate themselves in the most outlandish ways. Dressing up in unusual ways helps them to feel like brand-new people. This is an activity that will really get them in shape.

MATERIALS

Fabric scraps
String or yarn

ROOM ARRANGEMENT

Open space

TIME

30 minutes

DIRECTIONS

1. For this game, collect as many fabric scraps as you can — the more the better.

2. Push all the furniture to the corners of the room to create an open space. Place the fabric scraps and string in the center of the space.

3. Have each person pick a body part to transform using fabric scraps. To get started, suggest that they can wrap and stuff fabric to create cone-heads, huge clown feet, great muscular arms, and fat stomachs. Fabric might be wrapped around limbs or tied on with string. Coats and jackets can be worn over new body shapes to complete the transformation.

4. After these creatures have been created, organize a parade through the room, or ask the children to dance a slow-motion ballet.

BANNER TOGETHER

Banners are often used to proclaim the identity of individuals or groups. This activity allows individuals to express themselves by collaborating in making a group banner.

MATERIALS

Assorted colored felt rectangles approximately 9″ x 12″, one for each player
Fabric scraps, leftover ribbing, sequins, buttons, and so forth
Scissors
White glue
Assorted colored felt-tipped markers
Stapler
Safety pins
40″ dowel or strip of wood

ROOM ARRANGEMENT

Work area for every five or six players

TIME

40 to 60 minutes

DIRECTIONS

1. Before the activity begins, cover work tables with newspaper. Divide the players into groups of five or six. Give each player a felt rectangle. Supply each group with several pairs of scissors, a container or two of white glue, a few felt-tipped markers, and an assortment of fabric scraps and other decorative materials.

2. Since this banner is a symbol of the group as a whole, each person should be free to make a picture or design which expresses his or her own feelings and ideas. One may want to make an intricate design with lots of small details while another may want to make a very literal picture of some object. Whatever players decide upon, they must cut it out of the materials available and glue it to their felt rectangle. Felt-tipped markers should be used for outlining, highlighting, and adding mottoes.

3. Staple several felt pieces together in a row. When several equal rows of felt rectangles are connected, finish assembling them into a larger banner with safety pins. To hang the banner, staple or tack one end to a wooden dowel or piece of wood.

4. After the banner is finished, hang it from the ceiling or against the wall. The group can use the banner to head special parades and show off group spirit.

TACK BANNER TO A PIECE OF WOOD AND HANG WITH SCREW EYES AND STRING

STAPLE OR PIN FELT PIECES TOGETHER

OUTER FACES

Our faces tell many stories. In this activity, your group can enlarge upon facial communication with the help of a little theatrical makeup.

MATERIALS

Bottles of assorted colored water-based theatrical makeup
Plastic cups for makeup and water
Small inexpensive brushes *or* a supply of cotton-tipped swabs
Mirrors
Cold cream

ROOM ARRANGEMENT

Groups of 5 chairs

TIME

25 to 30 minutes

DIRECTIONS

1. Divide the players into groups of five. Give each group a cup and brush or swab for each makeup color. Pour ¼″ of paint into each cup. Although this activity is easy to motivate, it can become disorganized easily if not supervised. Try to get players to keep colors and brushes separated or colors will become muddy.

2. Before players begin to transform themselves, they must decide upon expressions to paint on their faces — happy, sad, angry, surprised, scared, and so on. Players must not tell each other which expressions they have chosen. You can help players by discussing expressions, how each one is different and what each communicates — furrowed brows, wrinkled noses, and so forth. Have them experiment by making faces in a mirror. Makeup will wash off more easily if players apply cold cream under the makeup.

3. After face painters are finished, gather them in a circle seated on the floor. One by one, players show off their faces and may even act out the emotion they are intending to communicate. This is a good opportunity for everyone to ham it up.

4. After the activity has ended, players should have the option to keep the makeup on or wash it off. Theatrical makeup will dry and should not come off on furniture, but may rub off on clothing.

Lights, Camera, Action

SLIDE MURALS

With a slide projector to help them execute a group mural, young artists will be able to create a masterpiece faster than you can say "Post-Impressionism."

MATERIALS

A sheet of 8½" x 11" paper for each player
A pencil for each player
Assorted colored felt-tipped markers
Masking tape
A slide of an object (an animal, a flower, a building, and so forth)
A slide projector, preferably one with a wide angle lens

ROOM ARRANGEMENT

Open space

TIME

45 minutes

DIRECTIONS

1. Find a slide of something with lots of detail such as an animal, a flower, a building, a person's face — anything. A close-up picture with well-defined shapes works best.

2. Project the slide on a large flat surface — a wall or chalkboard — positioning the projector so that the image is as big as possible.

3. Cover the projected area with sheets of paper, tacking the edges of each sheet with tape. Each person should have his or her own sheet of paper, so if you have a big group or a small room, you may have to do this in several shifts.

4. Have each person trace his or her portion of the projected image with a pencil. Remind artists not to add any extra lines.

5. After completing the tracing, artists should remove their sheets from the wall and begin to fill in the lines with colors and shapes.

6. When everyone is finished, reassemble the mural, replacing the sheets in their original order.

SHADOW SHAPES

In this activity, players become shady characters doing gymnastics to help their shadows get into shape.

MATERIALS

Large roll of white paper (at least 36″ wide)
Thumb tacks *or* masking tape
Assorted colored felt-tipped markers
Assorted colored tempera paint
Brushes
Bucket of water
4 to 6 spotlights or the light from a slide projector

ROOM ARRANGEMENT

Open wall space

TIME

35 to 45 minutes

PAIRS OF PLAYERS TRACE EACH OTHERS SHADOW

DIRECTIONS

1. Tack or tape a roll of white paper across a wall. Pull shades and close doors to make the room as dark as possible. Plug in spotlights or slide projector and direct the light toward the paper.

2. Divide the group into pairs. Partners take turns tracing each other's shadows with felt-tipped markers on the white paper. Players should turn, stretch, and crouch to see how many different shapes they can make with just their bodies. Several pairs of players can stand together to merge silhouettes.

3. Spotlights can be moved to elongate, enlarge, or shrink shapes. For example, finger shadows can stretch out several feet across the wall. Suggest players trace the same shadow shape several times, overlapping it in different colors.

4. Players fill in the shapes with solid colors of tempera paint or with patterns such as stars, stripes, checks, dots, and so forth.

FILL IN SHAPES WITH COLORS AND PATTERNS

SPECIAL EFFECTS

This activity creates spectacular effects instantly with the help of a simple record player. Children love it.

AS PAPER PLATE SPINS BEGIN TO SLOWLY PULL MARKER FROM CENTER

MATERIALS

Several record players
Masking tape
Felt-tipped markers with broad tips
2 or 3 white paper plates for each player

ROOM ARRANGEMENT

Open space near an electrical outlet

TIME

25 minutes

DIRECTIONS

1. Put record players on a table, taping the sound arms out of the way. Leave enough space around the table for a crowd of onlookers. Keep felt-tipped markers in a central area for players to share. Give each player a paper plate.

2. Players fit paper plates on turntables by punching holes through them with record spindles. They turn on the record players and draw a design while the plates are spinning. Because the plates are in motion, very little hand motion is necessary. To create a spiral effect, begin in the middle and slowly pull the marker outward.

3. Have players remove their plates from the turntable and add to the designs. Parts can be colored and decorated with stars, stripes, and dots. Later, when designs are finished, place plates back on the turntable and watch the effects.

4. Because drawing on the turntable is so much fun, players will want to use plate after plate. Limit the number of plates each player may use. Ambitious inventors may want to cut their plates into three-dimensional spirals, combining several plates into one twirling sculpture.

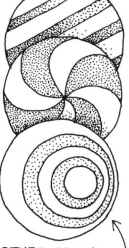

OTHER OPTICAL EFFECTS

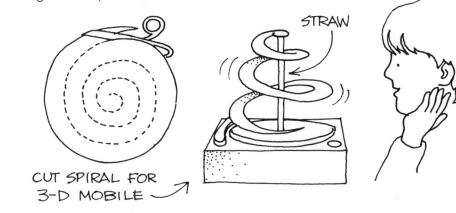

CUT SPIRAL FOR 3-D MOBILE

STRAW

JAM SESSION

You don't have to own a fancy grand piano or even play the guitar to be a musician. In this activity, common everyday materials become instrumental in a do-it-yourself orchestra.

MATERIALS

Wooden dowels, 3 feet long, ½-inch diameter
Hand saw
Heavy cardboard tubes (from business machine paper rolls)
Shoe boxes
Blocks of wood, 2" x 4" x 6"
Sheets of medium-weight sandpaper
White glue
Small boxes with lids
Paper lunch bags
Rubber bands
An assortment of beads, buttons, pebbles, marbles, and so on

ROOM ARRANGEMENT

As is

TIME

45 to 60 minutes

DIRECTIONS

1. Gather materials on a table. These simple instruments can be made quickly.

• *Rhythm Sticks* Cut a 3-foot dowel into three 1-inch sticks. Seven 3-foot dowels make enough sticks for ten players. To play, simply hit one stick against the other. For an extra sound, make grooves on one stick and rub with an unnotched stick.

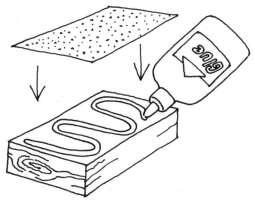

RHYTHM BLOCKS
Glue sandpaper to two pieces of wood and rub together

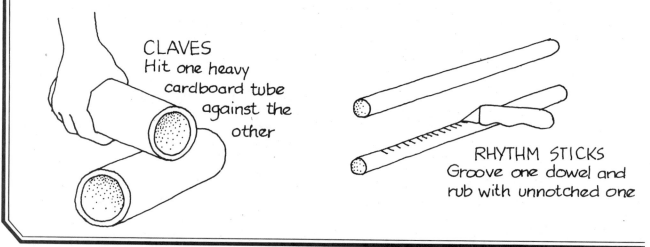

CLAVES
Hit one heavy cardboard tube against the other

RHYTHM STICKS
Groove one dowel and rub with unnotched one

- *Claves* Originally, claves were made from the trunk of a young tree. For this orchestra, use heavy cardboard tubes from business machine paper. To play, simply hold one tube and hit with the other.
- *Rhythm Blocks* Any wood scraps can be cut into rhythm blocks. For an added sound, glue a sheet of medium sandpaper on one side of each block and shuffle off. Each player will need two blocks.
- *Maracas* Fill small boxes and paper lunch bags with buttons, beads, marbles, and pebbles. Secure with rubber bands and shake.

2. Each player selects an instrument. Divide the group into three sections. With the leader conducting, ask the first section to beat out a rhythm. While the first section continues, the second section begins to beat out a counter rhythm. Both sections continue as the third section adds another rhythm. Each section takes a turn changing its rhythm while the other sections adjust their tempos accordingly.

3. Divide the group into two orchestras. The two groups face each other. The object is for each orchestra to "talk" to the other using the instruments. Taking turns, one group beats out about fifteen or twenty seconds of sound — shaking maracas, hitting rhythm sticks, and rubbing blocks. The other group reacts by playing back, either in a calm even tone or with frantic excitement.

4. Finish with a big finale using voices and other sounds. It is surprising how well inexperienced musicians can organize sounds and rhythms into a spontaneous symphony.

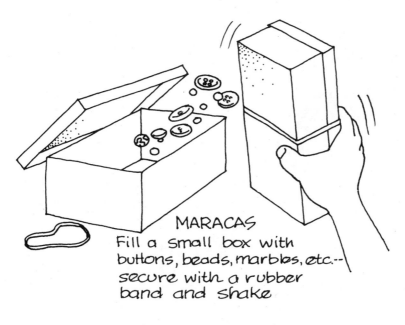

MARACAS
Fill a small box with buttons, beads, marbles, etc.-- secure with a rubber band and shake

VIDEO HIDE AND SEEK

Most of the time, people cannot wait to see themselves on a videoscreen. In this game, however, players will want to avoid it at all costs.

MATERIALS

Videocamera, recorder, and monitor
Videotape

ROOM ARRANGEMENT

Open space

TIME

10 minutes

DIRECTIONS

1. Set video equipment at one end of the room with camera and monitor facing players. Give players as much room as possible to be active. The object of the game is to try to escape the watchful camera lens without actually hiding behind furniture or objects.

2. Players gather at one end of the room. You slowly pan the room as players watch the monitor. Players must try *not* to be on screen and must rely on fast footwork — ducking, crawling, dodging, and so forth.

3. As players begin to wear themselves out, focus on a few of the least successful players. After players have calmed down, play the tape. Exhausted players won't care who wins or loses, but will enjoy their own slapstick antics.

EARTHQUAKE

When it comes to watching television, most people just sit passively. In this videogame no one will be able to sit at all.

MATERIALS

Videocamera, recorder, and monitor
Videotape

ROOM ARRANGEMENT

Open space

TIME

10 minutes

DIRECTIONS

1. Set video equipment at one end of the room with monitor facing away from players. Players sit, stand, talk, and act as if nothing were happening. (In a large group, divide players into groups of eight or ten so that everyone can be on the screen at once.)

2. As the videotape is recording the calm activities of the players, yell "Earthquake!" and start to shake the camera. Players begin to scream, shake, and fall down dramatically until no one is left standing.

3. After each group has recorded its "earthquake," play the tape.

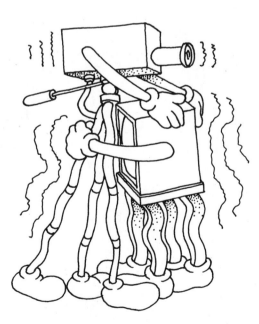

LIP SERVICE

This game is like Lip Sync (page 24) except that players record their dubbing on videotape.

MATERIALS

Videocamera, recorder, and monitor
Videotape

ROOM ARRANGEMENT

Open space

TIME

25 minutes

DIRECTIONS

1. Divide the players into groups of four. Each player should get a turn to play both roles — on-camera actor and off-camera talker.
2. The on-camera players act out a pantomime conversation (see Lip Sync, page 24) while the two other players stand off camera and fill in the words.
3. Limit each group to three minutes on camera. After several performances, play the tape.

SHOW-OFF

Here's a game where making faces is the rule rather than the exception.

MATERIALS

Videocamera, recorder, and monitor
Videotape

ROOM ARRANGEMENT

Open space

TIME

10 minutes

DIRECTIONS

1. Players take turns making faces in front of the camera. Each person looks directly into the lens for ten seconds and is allowed to make his or her silliest face.
2. Between silly faces, turn off the recorder so that only the players' best looks will be captured.
3. After the group is finished, players will have to face facts and watch the tape being played. For added silliness, record some lively music on the video sound track.

NO KIDDING

It's hard enough keeping a straight face when you're put on the spot, but being recorded on videotape will surely crack players up.

MATERIALS

Videocamera, recorder, and monitor
Videotape

ROOM ARRANGEMENT

Open space

TIME

15 minutes

DIRECTIONS

1. Players take turns staring into the camera lens without a sign of expression for fifteen seconds. Meanwhile, the rest of the group is off camera, trying to make the on-camera player laugh.

2. Off-camera players can make faces and sounds, but they may not touch the on-camera player. Turn off the recorder between takes so that only the serious stares of players will be shown.

3. The videotape is replayed so that stone-faced players will have a chance to laugh at themselves.

BRAGGING

We've each got something special to boast about, some incredible accomplishment or exciting experience. Here's a game where blowing one's own horn can turn the group into a band of braggers.

MATERIALS

Videocamera, recorder, and monitor
Videotape

ROOM ARRANGEMENT

Open space

TIME

30 to 45 minutes

DIRECTIONS

1. Players come before the camera, say their names, and tell the best things about themselves. For example, "I can play the piano with my eyes closed" or "I made the world's largest chocolate chip cookie — and ate it!" After each remarkable accomplishment, the rest of the group should give on-camera players a cheer. Limit each story to one minute.

2. After the last brag, sit everyone down and play the tape of the most wonderful group of players in the world.

Boxing

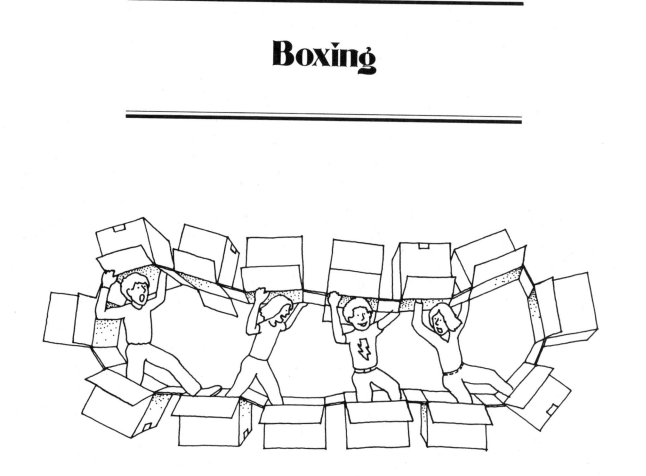

TUNNELS

The easiest of all arches to make is the three-box arch which, architecturally speaking, isn't actually an arch, but a lintel. Whatever it is, it is easy to make and can be made quickly. If many are placed side to side, the tunnel is born.

MATERIALS
50 to 75 cardboard boxes

ROOM ARRANGEMENT
Open space

TIME
25 minutes

DIRECTIONS
1. Close flaps on the boxes by overlapping them. Decide with the group how long and what shape the tunnel should be. Tunnels can be straight or they can wind, spiral, and snake.
2. After some design agreements have been made, players should stack two parallel rows of boxes with enough space between them for players to crawl. Then they can put boxes on top to cover it. Suggest that players leave top boxes off for skylights or that they build small individual-sized niches off the main tunnel.
3. Even before the tunnel is finished, players will begin crawling in and out. Be careful, however, of players crawling on top of the tunnel while others are inside.
4. Tunnels can be even more fun when they are connected to secret rooms or other constructions, like fabric-covered tents. Tunnels can be used as part of other games and activities, such as Follow-the-Leader.

STACKING THE DECK

Activities are not always defined by rules — some are defined by materials. In this activity, players explore materials and the games occur spontaneously. When players stack boxes, far more is happening than is obvious. They are structuring the play process. This activity is an exercise in creative play and, although there are specific directions, the leader's role is more responsive than directive.

MATERIALS

50 to 75 cardboard boxes

ROOM ARRANGEMENT

Open space

TIME

25 minutes

DIRECTIONS

1. Close boxes by overlapping flaps. Stack them in a pile in the center of the room.

2. Allow players a short time for an initial investigation. Soon players will welcome some direction. Organize the activity by suggesting a wall be built to divide the room.

3. You can assist building, but players will stack the boxes rapidly and enthusiastically. As the wall is being built, players will be on either side walling in or out other players. Hide-and-seek games will soon occur as players play peek-a-boo through the spaces. Continue to direct the overall structure and encourage self-motivated play by having players build the wall as high as possible.

4. After players have built the wall, it inevitably will be knocked down so the process can begin again. In the interest of safety and box conservation, it is best to anticipate this part of the play cycle. Organize a collapsing game with players slowly taking boxes away from the bottom.

5. When boxes have fallen, quickly reorganize everyone by suggesting a more specific challenge — the creation of a large arch. Making an arch out of boxes demands total cooperation and means understanding the nature of the keystone. The keystone is the central box at the crown of the arch which holds all the other boxes in place. To construct the arch all players will have to hold boxes in the air until the keystone can be set in place.

6. The success of the cooperative arch will provide a positive atmosphere in which players can organize themselves in other self-motivated projects.

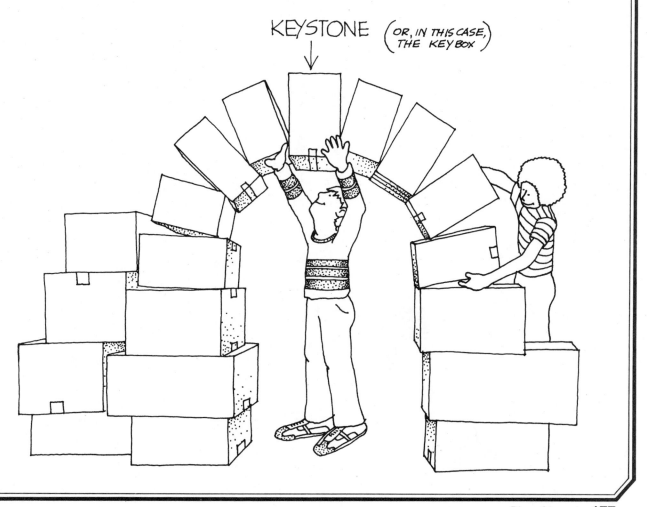

KEYSTONE (OR, IN THIS CASE, THE KEY BOX)

BOX LINKS

When the flaps of two boxes are joined together, the result is a building unit with infinite possibilities.

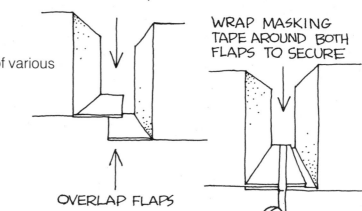

WRAP MASKING TAPE AROUND BOTH FLAPS TO SECURE

OVERLAP FLAPS

MATERIALS

60 to 80 cardboard packing boxes of various sizes
Masking tape

ROOM ARRANGEMENT

Open space

TIME

30 to 40 minutes

DIRECTIONS

1. Divide players into groups of five or six. Give each group about 15 boxes and a roll of masking tape.

2. In this activity the flaps of boxes are taped together into a hinge that creates a flip-flop module. To tape flaps, bring two boxes together and overlap flaps. Wrap masking tape around both flaps to secure.

3. Since one box has as many as eight flaps, the possibilities of connecting it to other boxes are endless. Boxes can be connected into a single snaking line, a tank tread, or a complex cluster. Help players get started by demonstrating various possibilities. Two groups might want to work together on one gigantic box chain.

4. When every box has been linked, allow some time for everyone to play with the many variations made by the hinges. Box chains might become rocket ships or trains. Changing them into other shapes will take cooperation and some inventive planning. When players seem to be finished testing their box constructions, store them for later use.

BOXING MATCH

There's no fighting in this game — just a creative battle of wits. With this activity, players not only make their own puzzle, but also try to figure out how it fits together.

MATERIALS

9 cardboard boxes of similar size
Paint cups
Brushes
Tempera paint in assorted colors
Bucket of water
Sponge or mop
Newspapers
Pencils

ROOM ARRANGEMENT

Open space

TIME

45 minutes

DIRECTIONS

1. Divide the players into nine groups. Give each group a cardboard box, assorted colors of tempera paint in cups, several brushes, and some newspaper to cover the floor. Keep a bucket of water and a sponge or mop close by for cleanup.

2. Assemble the boxes in the middle of the floor, flush against each other in three rows of three. The object of the activity is to draw a large picture on the combined surfaces of all nine boxes. Have players choose a simple design or object to draw — a face, flower, house, or geometric design. Give pencils to two or three players to draw a simple outline of the design over all nine boxes.

3. When the drawing is finished, turn the boxes to a clean side and have two or three different players draw another picture. Repeat the large outline drawings until all six sides of each box have a different design.

4. Next, have each group paint all six sides of its box in any manner it chooses — as long as each outline and design is followed.

5. When paintings are dry, reassemble them into one of the six pictures. Allow players time to rearrange the blocks into the six different pictures or invent new ones by mixing the designs.

DRAW A DESIGN OVER ALL 9 BOXES

TURN BOXES AND DRAW DESIGNS UNTIL ALL SIDES ARE FILLED

AMAZING BOXES

Mazes are at least as old as the Minotaur myth and as recent as the fun house at the amusement park. People of all ages enjoy the adventure of trying to find their way out of a labyrinth. In this activity players lose themselves not only in a maze but also in the process of building it.

MATERIALS

50 to 75 cardboard boxes of various sizes
Tempera paint in assorted colors
5 brushes for every three players
5 paint cups for every three players
Bucket of water
Masking tape
A pencil for each player
Newspapers

ROOM ARRANGEMENT

Open space

TIME

45 to 60 minutes

DIRECTIONS

1. Divide players into groups of three. Give each group several boxes, five cups of paint in various colors, a brush for each color, several pencils,

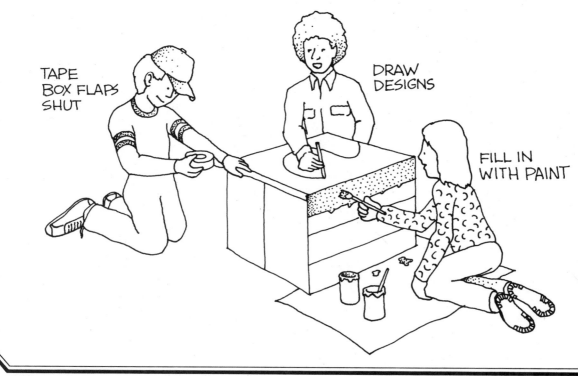

TAPE BOX FLAPS SHUT

DRAW DESIGNS

FILL IN WITH PAINT

and masking tape to share with other groups. Pass around sheets of newspaper so that players can cover the floor.

2. Before the mazes are created, decorate the boxes with signs and symbols. Players tape the boxes shut with masking tape and then draw outlines of designs. Directional elements, such as arrows, can be used in the maze to send players in different directions. Words, such as "Danger" or "Enter at your own risk!" add mystery to the maze. Other decorative elements, such as stars, dots, and patterns, can be added for the eye-catching fun of it.

3. When every box is painted and dry, players can arrange the boxes into a maze. Players stack boxes into a confusing network of hidden routes and dead-end passages. Boxes should be piled high enough so that players moving through the maze cannot see other players and cannot tell where the passage leads. Parts of the maze can be enclosed with other boxes to create dark, mysterious chambers.

4. Playing with the maze is the most fun. Older children will enjoy the decorating and the construction while smaller children will be happy just to crawl around. Young children enjoy having you pretend to be a dragon or a monster.

5. After this activity, store the decorated boxes for fast fun — over and over again.

NICE BIG DICE

The making of very big dice leads to the creation of very big games with very big stakes.

MATERIALS

2 cube-shaped cardboard boxes of similar size
Masking tape
Black felt-tipped marker

ROOM ARRANGEMENT

Open space

TIME

30 minutes

DIRECTIONS

1. Tape box flaps securely shut with masking tape. Add dots with a black felt-tipped marker. On a traditional die the numbers on opposite faces always add up to 7. (If you would like to make fancy dice, paint the boxes with white acrylic paint before applying dots.)

2. To throw oversized dice, clear the area. On the count of three, toss. One tosser for each die is usually best. Big dice are very theatrical and can make any game in which dice are required a special game.

Chip Off the Old Box

1. If lots of boxes have been collected for other activities, use them as big playing "chips."

2. Divide the group into two teams.

3. When a team rolls a 7 or a double, it gets a box. A team that throws 11 must forfeit one box to the other team.

4. The team that collects all the boxes is the winner.

Ten Steps

1. Divide the group into two teams — one "odd" and the other "even."

2. Divide the room in half with a line of masking tape on the floor.

3. Have each team line up ten steps behind its side of the line.

4. If the odd team throws 3, 5, 7, 9, or 11, all team members take one step toward the goal. If the even team throws 4, 6, 8, 10, or 12, all team members may take one step forward. If odd throws even or even throws odd, nobody moves. If either team throws a 2 (snake eyes), team members must retreat one step.

5. The first team to reach the center of the room is the winner.

54

1. This game requires two teams of fifteen players. Each team gets one die. The object is to throw the die fifteen times and get 54 points or as close as possible to 54 without going over. (If there are twenty players, change the game to ten rounds and 36 points.)

2. Both teams stand in line. The leader says "Go" and the first players on each team throw their die into the center of the room. All players take a turn throwing their team's die.

3. Scores are added up. If a team gets 55 or more points, it loses. If teams tie, they both win.

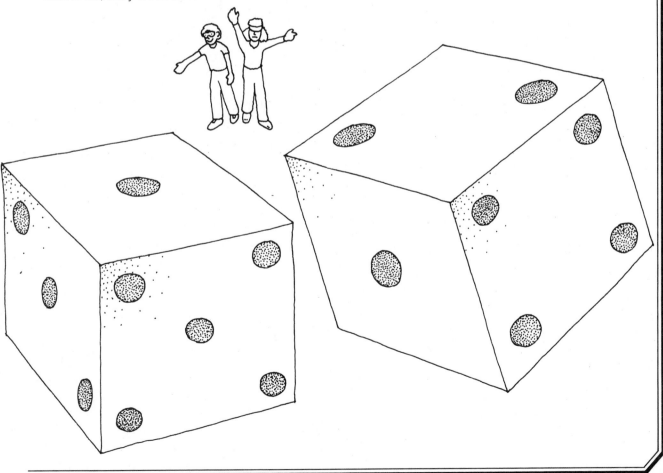

SHOE-BOX DOMINOES

In the traditional game of dominoes, players try to match the number of dots on one tile with the number of dots on another. While serious domino players in one room are mulling over their moves, others are in another room, building a long line of dominoes standing on end, giving the last one in line a little nudge, and enjoying the spectacle of a domino chain reaction as the tiles topple. This game replaces the small domino tiles with a shoe-box spectacular.

MATERIALS

As many shoe boxes as possible (at least 100)
Newspapers
Tempera paint in assorted colors
A paint cup for each player
A brush for each player
Masking tape

ROOM ARRANGEMENT

Open space

TIME

60 minutes

DIRECTIONS

1. Ask everyone in the group to help collect shoe boxes for this spectacular.
2. Since this is not a traditional domino game, shoe boxes can be decorated with all kinds of colors and designs. First, tape box tops to box bottoms. To decorate, separate the group into three teams, each with an equal number of shoe boxes. Divide paint supplies among the groups. Each person can paint one box at a time or players can pass the boxes down an assembly line on newspaper sheets with each person adding one small design.

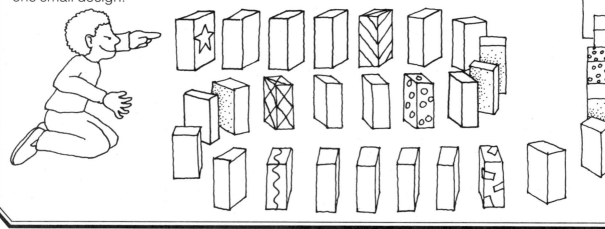

3. Once all boxes are dry, it's time to test out some falling formations.

- *Snake* The Snake is the most basic. Stand boxes on end in a curving line. Boxes on the inside of the turn almost touch each other to insure proper toppling.
- *Tree* The Tree is a line of boxes which branches off into more lines. Having one box hit two other boxes will set off two other lines. Each of those lines can split off into other lines, and so forth.
- *Whirlpool* The Whirlpool is a double spiral. To create a spiral, turn boxes in a continuous curve that gets smaller toward the center. At the center, turn the spiral out in reverse, placing the reverse spiral between the lines of the other spiral. Some adjustment may have to be made to leave room between the lines.
- *Fireworks* Fireworks uses spirals combined with a Tree. Begin with a straight line at the end of which one box hits two other boxes. The two boxes set off two spirals. More Fireworks can be added by having spirals branch off other spirals.
- *Figure 8* In the Figure 8, the shoe-box lines crisscross. Where one line crosses another, be sure to leave a large enough gap so that falling boxes do not accidentally hit the intersecting line.

4. After a few trial runs and some experimentation with some other formations, everyone should be ready for the Giant Shoe-Box Domino Spectacular. Have each group set up a domino design, curving boxes around furniture and under tables and twisting lines into geometric patterns. Groups should find ways to connect their designs into one big domino fall. Draw a name for the Official Shoe-Box Toppler and then have a mass countdown.

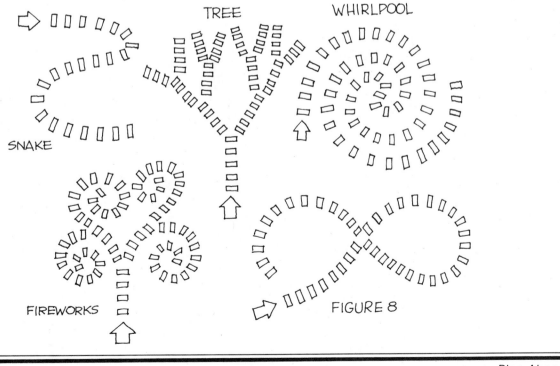

BOXED IN

There's nothing square about costumes made from boxes. With a little labor and some imagination, boxes can become robots, cars, birds, and fishes. Here are a few box steps to help move players in the right direction.

MATERIALS

Boxes of assorted sizes, one for each player
Utility knife
Newspapers
Masking tape
A pencil or felt-tipped marker for each player
A paint cup for each player
A brush for each player
Miscellaneous pieces of cardboard, small boxes, paper plates, and so forth

ROOM ARRANGEMENT

Open space

TIME

60 minutes

DIRECTIONS

1. Before the activity begins, prepare boxes by cutting holes for heads, arms, and bodies. Move furniture to the edges of the room. Protect the floor by covering it with newspaper.

2. Place precut boxes in a pile in the center of the room. Keep paints centrally located on one table, allowing players to take and return one cup of paint at a time.

3. Each player selects a box. Before players begin to paint, discuss box-costume designs, listing an assortment of possibilities from dragons to flying saucers.

4. Players draw in designs first with pencils — outlining feathers, flowers, lights, scales, or whatever — before filling in with paint. Additional pieces of cardboard, small boxes, and paper plates can be cut and taped on for eyes, heads, feet, wings, tails, and so forth.

5. Completed box costumes can be displayed in a fashion show or can be the basis for improvised skits.

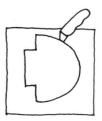

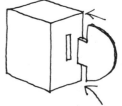

CUT EARS, WINGS AND FINS FROM SCRAP PIECES -- SLOT AND SLIP INTO PLACE

FUN CITY

This may be the only opportunity students will have to design a world where having fun is the only job.

MATERIALS

6 to 10 appliance boxes (from refrigerators, washing machines, and so forth)
Felt-tipped markers
Tempera paint in assorted colors
A paint cup for each player
A brush for each player
Bucket of water
Newspapers

ROOM ARRANGEMENT

Open space

TIME

60 minutes

DIRECTIONS

1. Clear the room of furniture and cover the floor with newspapers. Arrange boxes around the edges of the room, leaving enough space for construction. Collect paint supplies on one table.

2. With the group seated, discuss ways to design a city as if it were an amusement park and the major industry were making fun. Decide on the kinds of things each box will become. For example, one box might be called "Free Jokes" with a player hidden inside ready to pop out with a joke for a needy caller. Other boxes might be filled with strange sounds, small holes for peeking, free fortunes, and even a "House of Horrors."

3. Divide the class into groups of three or four for each building. Players should agree on the design and begin to outline doors, windows, and any other opening that needs to be cut. (You should cut openings yourself with a utility knife.)

4. Keep all paint supplies in one spot. Have players take a brush and one cup of paint at a time and return later for refills and other colors. They can clean paint-soaked brushes in the bucket of water.

5. As the residents of Fun City finish decorating their fun buildings with bright colors and whimsical designs, move the boxes into place. When the paint is dry have the Funites (as they are called) get to work raising fun.

ABOUT THE AUTHOR

As an artist and graphics designer, Bob Gregson has created playful
programs for more than 10 years. He's directed the art classes for the
Wadsworth Atheneum in Hartford, Connecticut; taught at the Young Artists
Studios in Chicago; and designed participatory programs and exhibits for
the Art Institute of Chicago and the Capital Children's Museum in
Washington, D.C. As cofounder of Sidewalk, Inc. in Hartford, Bob helped
organize a yearly Play Day, a large-scale community festival which is a
model of collective creativity. He developed the Activity Truck, a mobile
playground which transforms neighborhoods into festivals in an instant.
Bob has produced inventive media events for television and radio and is
currently working as the Cultural Planner for the City of New Haven's Office
of Cultural Affairs, planning programs to make the city more fun.